Women of Letters

Studies in German Literature, Linguistics, and Culture

Edited by James Hardin
(*South Carolina*)

About *Women of Letters:*

In early nineteenth-century Germany, books composed of personal correspondence were a genre of choice among women writers. The epistolary works of the three authors represented here are studied for common features and for their individual contributions to the genre. *Caroline: Letters of Early Romanticism* is Caroline Schlegel-Schelling's attempt to define her intellectual role; Rahel Varnhagen's *Rahel: Book of Remembrance* is concerned with transforming epistolarity into metaphysical speculation; and Bettina von Arnim in *Goethe's Correspondence with a Child* uses the form to produce an idealized account of Romantic love. All offer valuable insights on the sender-recipient relationship, the presentation of a "self," the effect of foreknowledge of publication on a correspondence, and editing for a wider public.

Margaretmary Daley is Assistant Professor of German at Case Western Reserve University.

Margaretmary Daley

Women of Letters

A Study of Self and Genre in the Personal Writing of Caroline Schlegel-Schelling, Rahel Levin Varnhagen, and Bettina von Arnim

Camden House

Copyright © 1998 Margaretmary Daley

All Rights Reserved. Except as permitted under current legislation, no part of this work may be photocopied, stored in a retrieval system, published, performed in public, adapted, broadcast, transmitted, recorded, or reproduced in any form or by any means, without the prior permission of the copyright owner.

First published 1998
Camden House
Drawer 2025
Columbia, SC 29202–2025 USA

Camden House is an imprint of Boydell & Brewer Inc.
PO Box 41026, Rochester, NY 14604–4126 USA
and of Boydell & Brewer Limited
PO Box 9, Woodbridge, Suffolk IP12 3DF, UK

ISBN: 1–57113–132–9

Library of Congress Cataloging-in-Publication Data

Daley, Margaretmary, 1961-
 Women of letters : a study of self and genre in the personal writing of Caroline Schlegel-Schelling, Rahel Levin Varnhagen, and Bettina von Arnim / Margaretmary Daley.
   p.   cm. – (Studies in German literature, linguistics, and culture (Unnumbered))
 Includes bibliographical references and index.
 ISBN 1-57113-132-9 (alk. paper)
 1. German letters -- Women authors -- History and criticism.
 2. German prose literature -- 19th century -- History and criticism.
 3. Schelling, Karoline Michaelis, 1763-1809 -- Correspondence.
 4. Varnhagen, Rahel, 1771-1833 -- Correspondence. 5. Arnim, Bettina von, 1785-1859 -- Correspondence. 6. Authors, German -- 19th century -- Correspondence. I. Title. II. Series.
PT811.D35
836'.6099287—dc21   98-6066
                                                            CIP

This publication is printed on acid-free paper.
Printed in the United States of America

Contents

Acknowledgments	vii
Introduction	ix
List of Abbreviations	xiv
1: Reading Published Correspondences: Gender, Genre, and the Self in Progress	1
2: Preserving the Self in Progress: Caroline Schlegel-Schelling	14
3: The Self from Ego to I: Rahel Levin Varnhagen	46
4: The Loving Self: Bettina von Arnim	74
Conclusion: The Self in Context	105
Bibliography	111
Index	129

Acknowledgments

In the early 1980s, as an undergraduate at Stanford University, I enrolled in Women's Studies courses offered by the French and English sections — seminars on French women poets and nineteenth-century British women's fiction — and I grew curious about the lack of comparable offerings in German, my chosen major. Suggestions to work on post-Second World War German literature, where women novelists were easy to find, only piqued my curiosity about the earlier periods, especially the late eighteenth and early nineteenth centuries. Katharina Mommsen encouraged me to explore the work of German women on my own, in what has become a lifelong project to discover these authors and make them accessible to others.

As I learned how much hard work was required to convert curiosity into scholarship, I incurred a tremendous debt of gratitude to my doctoral advisor, Cyrus Hamlin at Yale University. He encouraged my work with patience and persistence through a number of years in meetings from New Haven to Tübingen. To all my professors at Yale, I owe thanks for guidance and inspiration.

The research for this book was made possible by grants and fellowships from the German Academic Exchange Service (DAAD), the Faculty Development Center at Brigham Young University, and the W. P. Jones Faculty Development Fund at Case Western Reserve University. Because of the often precarious status of many historical women's letters, I have depended greatly on assistance given by the different staff members at the libraries where materials related to the published correspondences are archived, including the Goethe und Schiller Archiv in Weimar, the Deutsches Literaturarchiv in Marbach, the Staatsbibliothek in Berlin, and the Beinecke Rare Book and Manuscript Library in New Haven. At home at Case Western Reserve University, Michael Partington and N. Sue Hanson at the Kelvin Smith Library met all my needs — bibliographic and electronic. For all levels of assistance with the manuscript, my thanks go to David P. Benseler, to my colleagues at CWRU, my assistant, Eliezer Gurarie, and to James Hardin and his excellent staff at Camden House, especially Jim Walker.

On a personal level, I have to thank my family for supporting me and my project. My children Blake and Devin Ann have taught me to seek discipline in what I do without losing joy and excitement. Beyond words is my gratitude to my husband, Charlie.

M. M. D.
August 1998

Introduction

The early nineteenth century saw a flowering of writing by German women. In this period, one of the major forms of women's self-expression was the book of literary letters. This study concerns the published letters of three remarkable women from the German Romantic period, Caroline Schlegel-Schelling (1763–1809), Rahel Varnhagen (1771–1833), and Bettina von Arnim (1785–1859), women who advanced the boundaries of epistolary writing to explore the complexities and nuances of female self-definition.

In this study, I attempt to read the works of these three women as I believe they hoped they would be read, as literary works of self-discovery. Though current critics have begun to give these women's writings their proper due, generations of scholars read the letters as if they were primarily about history, about the literary culture of Jena and Berlin and the famous people who frequented the salons there. These women lived in dramatic times, when the Romantic revolution was transforming European culture, and all three ran literary salons in cultural centers — Schlegel-Schelling in Jena, Varnhagen and Arnim in Berlin — and they were confidantes to many of the central figures of German Romanticism like Friedrich and August Wilhelm Schlegel, Ludwig Tieck, Johann Wolfgang von Goethe, and Ludwig van Beethoven. (I use the term Romanticism as it is generally understood in English to refer to the international literary movement of the age of Goethe and his contemporaries, not in the more restrictive sense in which it is used by Germanists who apply it specifically to one particular phase of that period). In their letters, they left striking records of these times.

While the three women's letters provide fascinating accounts of their acquaintances with these famous people, one has only to turn to the letters themselves to see that these women writers were not selflessly devoted to chronicling the culture that surrounded them or the famous people who frequented their salons; first and foremost, the women were interested in themselves, in their personal experience, in the unfolding of their private lives, in self-discovery.

Caroline Schlegel-Schelling's letters were first published by Georg Waitz under the title *Caroline: Briefe an ihre Geschwister, ihre Tochter Auguste, die Familie Gotter, F. L. W. Meyer, A. W. und Fr. Schlegel, J. Schelling u. a. nebst Briefen von A. W. und Fr. Schlegel u. a.* (1871; Caroline: Letters to Her

Sister, Her Daughter Auguste, the Gotter Family, F. L. W. Meyer, A. W. and Fr. Schlegel, J. Schelling, etc., Together with Letters from A. W. and Fr. Schlegel). The letters leave a record of her life from girlhood through her marriages with August Wilhelm Schlegel and Friedrich Wilhelm Joseph Schelling, two key theorists of German Romanticism, and her struggle to define herself as a woman intellectual against the radical backdrop of the French Revolution.[1] Rahel Varnhagen's *Rahel: Ein Buch des Andenkens für ihre Freunde* (1833; Rahel: A Book of Remembrance for her Friends) describes the events of her life as a Jewish salon hostess in Berlin, but at its heart records the author's obsession with her self, her personal struggle against adversity, and attempts to reconcile her overwhelming pessimism with her yearning for sublime transcendence.[2] Bettina von Arnim's *Goethe's Briefwechsel mit einem Kinde: Seinem Denkmal* (1835; translated by Arnim et al. as *Goethe's Correspondence with a Child: For his Monument*, 1837–38) draws on letters from the author's friendship with the poet Goethe to produce an idealized expression of Romantic love.[3]

In the course of this study, I provide translations from Schlegel-Schelling and Varnhagen, which are the first time many of these passages have appeared in English. As is common in personal letters, the three women used grammar and punctuation informally and distinctively. Like the women's German editors, I have preserved in the translations the idiosyncratic mechanics of the manuscript letters. It is particularly important in translating Varnhagen and Arnim not to normalize the grammar because both authors frequently write in fragments, abrupt grammatical shifts, and unfinished thoughts. I have attempted to convey the distinctive, open-ended style of these authors in the translations. Unfortunately, because of the extent of the quotations, it was not expedient to provide texts in both German and English translations, and I have opted for translation alone. Only Arnim's work is available in English; Arnim herself and several collaborators translated the work in 1837–38, but this translation unfortunately suggests that Arnim's English style was not as exquisite as her German. While the original is written in expressive, generally colloquial German, the English translation often employs unnatural word order and other peculiarities like the use of the archaic *thou* to translate the German second person singular *du*. I have consulted Arnim's translation but not relied exclusively upon it. All three collections went through several German editions and have remained available in abridged form. Yet, in spite of their continued popularity, the current generation of feminist critics has only just begun the work of properly appreciating the letters of these women. As I have observed, generations of literary critics treated the works of Schlegel-Schelling, Varnhagen, and Arnim, as footnotes to the work of their famous literary intimates, Goethe, the Schlegels, and other members of the German Romantic movement.

A striking indication of their neglect is the current confusion over their names. Some critics refer to them by their maiden names — Caroline Michaelis, Rahel Levin, and Bettina Brentano — and others by their married names. Varnhagen and Arnim each had one husband (Karl August Varnhagen von Ense and Achim von Arnim), but Schlegel-Schelling had three (Johann Böhmer, August Wilhelm Schlegel, and Friedrich Wilhelm Joseph Schelling), and all three women were related by blood or marriage to men who played important roles in German Romanticism — Schlegel-Schelling's second and third husbands, Varnhagen's brother Ludwig (who used the pen name Ludwig Robert, hence references to Rahel Robert), and Arnim's brother Clemens Brentano and husband Achim von Arnim — so scholars often refer to the women by the last name of the relation they consider most prominent: sometimes the brother, sometimes one husband or another. The issue is further confused by common variant spellings, Karoline and Bettine. I refer to the names I judge to be used most frequently, which I hope scholars can ultimately agree upon as standard forms.

There are other reasons why many critics have not properly appreciated these correspondences as literary works of self-discovery. Because they originated in personal letter writing, they share some of the provisionalness and occasionality of a diary. In order fully to comprehend them, the reader must relish the slow pace and meandering narrative of authors like Pepys and Boswell. And, as I will explain, critics still have trouble grasping the genre of these works. Most readers want to place a work either in the category of fact or fiction. They experience frustration defining these letters because they do not fit neatly into either one of these categories. They are certainly not fictional, because they concern the women's historical lives. Yet to describe the letters as factual also misses the point. Arnim actually fictionalized aspects of her experience in her letters, rewriting many letters after the fact in order to idealize her exchange with Goethe. All three correspondences concern not facts alone but private, subjective experiences. A lyric poem may describe literal events in the author's life but we do not refer to it as a work of non-fiction. By the same token, these imaginative personal correspondences are properly considered not historical but literary works. This insistence may seem old fashioned, but, if we ignore it, we run the risk of failing to grasp the dramas of subjectivity and self-fashioning expressed within these women's letters.

By viewing the correspondences as literary artifacts of self-definition it is possible to appreciate the uniqueness of these women's voices and the lifelong evolution of an epistolary self. The writings of Varnhagen, Schlegel-Schelling, and Arnim share a thematic focus of great complexity: the act of defining a female self through personal letter writing — the quest for self-vision. It is the goal of this study to recover that vision.

Notes

[1] The first edition of Schlegel-Schelling's letters was published by a scholar, Georg Waitz, sixty-two years after her death: Caroline Schlegel-Schelling, *Caroline: Briefe an ihre Geschwister, ihre Tochter Auguste, die Familie Gotter, F. L. W. Meyer, A. W. und Fr. Schlegel, J. Schelling u. a. nebst Briefen von A. W. und Fr. Schlegel u. a.*, ed. Georg Waitz (Leipzig: Hirzel, 1871). Since then, there have been several editions (see bibliography), the majority consisting of selected letters. I quote from the most complete edition, *Caroline: Briefe aus der Frühromantik*, ed., Erich Schmidt, 2 vols. (Leipzig: Insel, 1913), which is based on Waitz's first edition, but contains additional unpublished letters and extensive annotations. To date, there has been no critical, historical edition.

[2] Varnhagen's letters first appeared immediately after her death, in manuscript form, selected and edited by her husband, Karl August Varnhagen von Ense: *Rahel: Ein Buch des Andenkens für ihre Freunde* (Berlin: 1833), and were published the next year. This edition contains only a part of her voluminous letter writing. There is much evidence that Varnhagen helped to prepare the edition before her death, though it is not possible to say definitively how much of the final editorial form was the work of her husband. Her literary estate contained thousands of letters not printed in the "Book of Remembrance," and many of these, including her correspondences with her husband, with David Veit, and Karoline von Humboldt, as well as her diaries, were published in the nineteenth century in various editions (see bibliography). Two more portions of her letters, her correspondences with Rebecca Friedländer and Pauline Wiesel, have only been published in the last ten years. Over the years, her letters have been available in several abridgements. The collected edition of her writings is Rahel Varnhagen, *Gesammelte Werke*, 10 vols., ed. Konrad Feilchenfeldt, Uwe Schweikert, and Rahel E. Steiner (Munich: Matthes, 1983), though this edition does not include the two most recent publications. To date there has been no critical, historical edition of the "Book of Remembrance," based on the extant manuscripts.

[3] The first edition was published by Arnim as *Goethe's Briefwechsel mit einem Kinde: Seinem Denkmal*, 3 vols. (Berlin: 1835). Arnim is the only one of the three women who published extensively, during her lifetime, and she herself published a collected works in 1853. Helmut Hirsch's bibliography, among others, lists her works, as well as the extensive posthumous publications of her letters and other writings. Her epistolary writings and other works have been collected in several major scholarly editions. When possible, I have used the most recent and extensively annotated *Werke und Briefe*, ed. Walter Schmitz and Sibylle von Steinsdorff, 3 vols. to date (Frankfurt am Main: Deutscher Klassiker, 1986–).

Abbreviations

BA: Bettine von Arnim, *Werke und Briefe*. Ed. Walter Schmitz and Sibylle von Steinsdorff. 3 vols. to date. Frankfurt: Deutscher Klassiker, 1986– .

CS: Caroline Schlegel-Schelling, *Caroline: Briefe aus der Frühromantik*. Ed. Erich Schmidt. 2 vols. Leipzig: Insel, 1913. Rpt. Berlin: Lang, 1970.

KFSA: Friedrich Schlegel. *Kritische Friedrich-Schlegel-Ausgabe*. 35 vols. Ed. Ernst Behler et al. Munich: Schöningh, 1958– .

RV: Rahel Levin Varnhagen, *Gesammelte Werke*. 10 vols. Ed. Konrad Feilchenfeldt, Uwe Schweikert, and Rahel E. Steiner. Munich: Matthes and Seitz, 1983.

1: Reading Published Correspondences: Gender, Genre, and the Self in Progress

This chapter concerns two major problems — gender and genre — and the claim that literary correspondence is uniquely suited for an exploration of the self in progress. These are important theoretical issues that need to be considered before examining the works of Schlegel-Schelling, Varnhagen, and Arnim. The general reader interested in an introduction to the works of these three women may wish to turn immediately to the author studies in chapters two, three, and four; this chapter is addressed primarily to scholars concerned with women's writing and desiring a systematic understanding of the genre of literary correspondence.

A reader today is not likely to need convincing that gender is important in the work of these three women. At the end of the twentieth century, we are fascinated with rediscovering the forgotten or neglected lives of women from the past. Our three authors dramatize women's struggles to find self-expression in a period in which they were not generally encouraged to pursue literary careers. Gender not only proscribed their social selves but also their literary selves. All three women were educated at home, never in a secondary school or university, a fact that put limits on their formal training in the canonical genres of the day. The genre of the literary correspondence can be seen as a solution to the problem of women's writing in the period, since, given their educational opportunities, although it might have been difficult for them to become neoclassical poets or dramatists, it was normal for them to write letters. Letter writing was a conventional attainment for contemporary women. Although all three works transcend the scope of conventional letter writing, all had their origins in social correspondence.

The importance of genre as an issue may not be so obvious. What I show in this chapter is that we need to come to an understanding of the genre of these works before we read them. Too frequently in the past, critics have misunderstood the correspondences because of an inadequate grasp of their genre. This may be surprising. Certainly, literary letters abound throughout history and are commonly read and studied by scholars. Nevertheless, a survey of what has been written about Schlegel-Schelling, Varnhagen, and Arnim shows that much of it concerns issues that, in my view, are based on a mistaken understanding of the generic nature of these works. In the past, critics treated them as historical documents and focused on nonliterary issues. For example, many critics read Arnim's letters as a literal transcription of her correspondence with Goethe. These critics frequently concerned themselves with historical-philological issues: the propriety of Arnim's flirtation with Goethe, the light the letters shed on Goethe's creativity. When it became known that Arnim rewrote the letters and attributed letters to Goethe that he never wrote, critics were scandalized; they censured Arnim's emendations and attempted to recover the original correspondence. Reading the letters, however, as imaginative writing, the whole question of historical accuracy becomes marginal. Although contemporary criticism has focused more properly on Arnim's creativity, there is still a tendency in the literature to approach the letters as documents of social history. Social, ethical issues are not unimportant in the correspondences, but they are not the only concerns, not even the most important ones. A reading that considers only the historical relationships behind the letters may miss their significance as literary works.

While the writing in these correspondences may be imaginative, it would also be mistaken to read them the same way one would read an epistolary novel or a work of fiction. They are not novels. They do not have plots, any more than the typical human life has a plot. The letters in the body of a published correspondence comprise a written narrative, but a narrative altogether different from that of conventional fiction. That epistolary narrative is the medium in which a literary self develops, and it has its own unique structure, patterns, and rhythms. Because the letters were sent episodically over many years, the narrative of personal subjectivity to which they give rise displays the story of a literary self indirectly rather than telling it outright. Each self-expression receives a reply, and each reply necessitates response and revision, so that over the course of a letter-exchange an elaborate process of self-expression and dialogue takes shape. Due to pressures from gendered social definitions of the self and the contradictions of identity and audience, these works give voice to a dynamic and conflict-laden individuality.

All the women in this study write, not simply to narrate their stories, but, more complexly, to discover an identity from the process of epistolary intercourse made public. It is this act of gaining self-vision that gives the three correspondences their coherence and power and justifies the struggle with their formal complexities.

The Gender Question — The Genre Question

In the work of the women correspondents, the problem of genre cannot be considered separately from the problem of gender. Although the lives of the women in many ways illustrate the waning power of traditional restrictions on women's public roles in the nineteenth century, nevertheless, tradition, education, and convention restricted access to canonical genres for these three literary women. It is important not to forget the powerful prejudices against women's letters that prevailed at the time Schlegel-Schelling, Varnhagen, and Arnim wrote and how these attitudes continued to characterize much critical writing until quite recently. In an article of 1980, "Ad /d Feminam: Women, Literature, and Society," Catharine R. Stimpson writes: "Yet most women writers have confronted a trivialization of their textual ambitions, whether they attribute this to divine displeasure, constricting social structures, or their own lacks . . . " (175). Each woman in this study had to confront this trivialization of her ambitions, though, as we shall see, each devised a very different response to the problem. The prejudices pertain both to genre and to gender. The relative lack of attention critics have afforded to correspondences of the Romantic period may be due to an insufficient appreciation of the generic complexity of the works, but it is also due to the common view that personal letters by women are less serious than the high art of the traditional male canon.

Readers of German were offered women's letters from the period studied here in affordable paperbacks like collections by Günther Jäckel from 1966 and by Katja Behrens from 1981. The popularity of these three women is indicated by the availability of their writing in German paperbacks. Of interest are also the selections from Schlegel-Schelling's letters published by Sigrid Damm in 1980 and from Varnhagen published by Marlis Gerhardt in 1983; both volumes are modernized selections different from the letters' first appearances in print. Similarly, Arnim's epistolary works are being reprinted in affordable and convenient paperback books by large houses with extensive distributions — hers are the most easily obtained and in their primary published form, and, with the establishment of the International Bettina von Arnim Society and its yearbook, her writing has received more critical discussion in German than that of the other two women. Readers whose only access to German women writers is in English now have a fine collection in *Bitter Healing: German Women Writers From 1700 to 1830: An Anthology* (Blackwell and Zantop).

Fortunately, historical and biographical books are also being published to redress the past deficiency of secondary studies. *German Women as Letter Writers* (French), *In the Shadow of Olympus* (Goodman and Waldstein), *German Women in the Eighteenth and Nineteenth Centuries* (Joeres and Maynes) are three such studies. Many others are included in the bibliography. However, the three women writers, who are treated here as equals, have not received an equal amount of critical attention, and for readers with limited German, there are proportionately fewer helpful secondary studies. On Schlegel-Schelling, there are recent articles by Barbara Becker-Cantarino, Sara Friedrichsmeyer, Janice Murray, and Heidi Thomann

Tewarson. On Varnhagen, there are English-language studies by Dagmar Barnouw, Elke Frederiksen, Katherine R. Goodman, Doris Starr Guilloton, Deborah Hertz, Hilde Spiel, Heidi Thomann Tewarson, and Liliane Weissberg. Critical articles on Arnim accessible to English readers abound; there are also two important books, a monograph by Edith Waldstein and a festschrift by Elke Frederiksen and Katherine R. Goodman. These studies belong among a growing literature of studies of women's epistolary writing, fueled at times by theoretical works by feminist scholars of English and comparative literature such as Janet Altman, Linda S. Kauffman, and Elizabeth MacArthur.

While recent publications of women's letters bolster the literary value and accessibility of both letter writing and writing by women, they have not undone the disrepute of years of earlier editions, and few recent selected editions are accompanied by good notes or scholarly apparatus. This prejudice against the correspondence form applies to the epistolary work of canonical authors such as Christian Gellert, Humboldt, Goethe, and Schiller, but it is more of a problem with the epistolary work of the women for whom it was the primary form.

In order to appreciate these works, one must first set aside the assumption that their generic marginality indicates mediocrity or a lack of complex literary expression. Because women often did not feel compelled to model their writing on canonical works of literature, it is necessary, if one wishes to consider women's writing in the Romantic period, to learn to read genres once thought to be marginal. Critics of many persuasions have assumed that the restrictions that limited these women to letters as a form of literary expression resulted in letters that are themselves of limited literary quality. This view no doubt explains the considerable neglect and even hostility that met these writings from the time they were composed until quite recently, with the notable exception of the feminist scholars from the early part of the century like Ricarda Huch, Irmgard Tanneberger, and Johanna Lürßen). Even critics inclined toward sympathy with these authors may assume that the genre of correspondence, because it was the only one available, was an inadequate means of literary expression or may place the emphasis solely on biography and social history.

I will argue firmly to the contrary: correspondence was a genre not only appropriate but uniquely suited to the talents of the letter writers considered in this study. While all the authors used the genre of correspondence as a means of discovering the self in progress, it was particularly appropriate and urgent for these women writers to do so, not only because letters were practically the only outlet for expression available to them, but because letters enabled depths of self-expression that might not have been possible in the more formal, conventional genres. For our authors, a private letter to a friend was a more intimate, more open forum for self-exploration than any of the more canonical literary forms might have been.

In straightforward traditional terms, the genre question can be answered for each of these women's works: *Caroline: Letters from Early Romanticism* approaches biography and *Rahel: A Book of Remembrance* borders on autobiography, while *Goethe's Correspondence with a Child* is subsumed under the category of the epistolary novel. The interpretations that follow augment and at times correct the readings that traditional approaches have yielded. Methodologically, an expansion of the kinds of categories possible precedes the act of interpretation and so appends the genre of correspondence to the literary canon, a genre with the potential for foreknowledge of publication or for postscriptural editorial writing. Other genre studies must accept flexible and overlapping terms. For example, biography and autobiography often allow that some letters are autobiographical and that some autobiographies are epistolary. One or both statements may pertain to the same literary work. However, the border between epistolary novels and non-fictional letters is comparatively rigid. It is either seen as the quintessential difference between the two types of writing, or it is cast as one of the most elusive concepts that literary theory strives to define. In this theoretical debate, the term correspondence is meant as a heuristic remedy for genre study, one that can accommodate varying degrees of chronology, intentionality, and fictionality without displacing the ostensible commonalities that these espistolary works share. As integrated, epistolary publications, correspondences are the artistic harvest of letter writing. Letter writing was of course an activity that well-off women in the period were not only permitted but expected and even encouraged to engage in. Letter writing normally was a conduit for social communication — perhaps a formalization of the polite conversation of the drawing room and salon, an important cultural institution, which Herbert Scurla, Deborah Hertz, and Peter Seibert have brought to the attention of scholars.

Epistolary production and salon conversation have a long and related history; all three of these women were also women of the salon. Women who ran literary salons reputedly excelled at making smooth transitions from one topic to another and from one speaker to another so that conversation was apparently seamless; yet the familiar letter captures this problematic, sometimes awkward moment for eternity. Liliane Weissberg reads Varnhagen's letter writing in this vein: "She describes her thoughts and feelings in a language that is full of exclamation marks, peculiar phrases, and foreign words; instead of using a guidebook or following standard rules for stylistic form, she simulates a kind of oral communication" ("Writing" 80). This letter writing simulates, according to Weissberg, oral communication. The selfsame hallmarks have struck other critical readers like Uwe Schweikert as peculiarly female: "Her pounding heart teaches us freedom — anarchic, erotic, improvisational, serene and yet moved. That this was only, could only be the language of a woman, Rahel herself knew and announced" (*RV* 10: 40). Schweikert then cites Varnhagen in confirmation. In fact, though, Varnhagen does not agree with Schweikert but says rather that her style is neither intrinsically masculine nor feminine. Although she sets up a hierarchy of her hypothetical speculations, I strongly disagree that there is something obviously and innately feminine about Varnhagen's prose. Schweikert, in the passage I have just quoted, claims that Varnhagen's style is essentially female, a style he characterizes as "serene and yet moved," a translation of Varnhagen's epigraph, "still und bewegt." But in her epigraph, Varnhagen does not refer to the female voice, alone. The epigraph is a quotation from the poet Hölderlin and characterizes poetry in general, not just poetry written by one sex or the other. As the author herself observes, "I admit that at first glance my pages do not have the appearance of coming from a woman; however, if one wants to ascribe them at second inspection to a man, than that seems even less likely." Varnhagen goes on to compare her writing to other neither-woman-nor-man authors such as Goethe and Shakespeare. Varnhagen anticipates, perhaps, Virginia Woolf's thesis that powerful writing is androgynous.

The problem of identifying an exclusively female style is one that has occupied recent critics without producing any simple solutions. Virginia Woolf once wrote, "A woman's writing is always feminine; it cannot help being feminine; at its best it is most feminine .... [T]he only difficulty lies in defining what we mean by feminine" (Showalter, "Feminist Criticism" 14). I find that each correspondent presents a very different version of "feminine" writing. Although at the same time I am not entirely convinced by Elke Frederiksen and Monika Shafi's application of Hélène Cixous's concept of *écriture féminine* to Arnim's work; this formulation seems rather narrow and prescriptive.

The connection between women's writing and the spontaneity of oral discourse seems deeply rooted. In this argument, letter writing imitates spoken language, and since European society and culture deemed spoken discourse acceptable for the female gender, women were able to excel at it compared to men. It is important, nonetheless, not to attribute a lack of artistry to women letter writers, who had been admonished to strive for an imitation of supposedly natural conversation in their writing. As Sandra Gilbert and Susan Gubar observe, like salon conversationalists, the female correspondents acquired their apparent "'ease' of 'written speech'" through arduous practice and prodigious training ("Ceremonies" 22). There was little natural about it. Noticing the contradiction inherent in the idea of "written speech" ought to point out the fact that such an understanding of letter writing is a logical contradiction, that the graceful writing of the salon hostess is neither natural nor easy to produce.

While I reject the idea that letter writing produced a categorically natural feminine writing, there is no question that the genre was accessible to women and gave them considerable artistic freedom. As Patricia Spacks explains, "inertia was a social possibility" for women for whom little else was possible; moreover, "the world might not only allow but actively encourage women — as it has never encouraged men — simply to wallow in their inner lives" (*Female Imagination* 177). While this possibility may hold true in certain genres, such as the diary, the letter seems in the time of Romanticism genuinely to have been equally accessible and equally acceptable for men and women. As Barbara Johnson notes, for the women of German Romanticism, the social status of the personal letter as a private form means that it is not and has not always been modeled on male discourse, and, consequently, the self that correspondence expresses is not a monstrous aberration from conformity to male standards (154). The social role of personal letters as a domestic product means that for men they are not "high" literature; thus, even men may be encouraged in their letters, in Spacks's phrase, quoted above, "to wallow in their inner lives." Even Goethe and Schiller, in their personal letters, may engage in intimacy and self scrutiny that would have been uncharacteristic in other genres. By restricting the texts to published personal letters, the study can synthesize a variety of personal epistolary narratives without losing sight of the diversity of selves within the unity of epistolary expression.

Women writers who wished to write in a recognizably female voice found the greatest degree of success outside of traditional genres. For writers in the Romantic era, correspondence offered new possibilities because it encouraged personal as opposed to objective or philosophic self-reflection. For these three German women Romantics in particular, correspondence offered even richer possibilities, for most felt cramped by rules of formal genres such as poetry and yet were not satisfied with informality and ephemerality of conversation. These letters were and still are vehicles for the literary expression of a creative female self.

With such issues as a framework, examination can begin to turn to the generic unity and thematic self-expression in the correspondences. Although they are the subject of several excellent studies, like those by Ricarda Huch, Hannah Arendt and Gisela Dischner, past critics have tended to use the letters as sources of biographical information. Of those who have gone beyond the biographical approach, many have been hampered by nonliterary misconceptions. Some focus on issues of morality, personality, or psychological judgments, while others treat the correspondences as epistolary novels, giving no attention to the unique and controversial problems of narrative and editorial coherence. Allied with a growing number of scholars who seek to go beyond traditional approaches, I argue that, while each correspondence in a sense creates its own rules, these three share in the act of creatively and actively defining a self that is indivisibly entwined with literary production.

Some literary critics have remarked on several of the intriguing aspects of letter writing without subordinating them to a categorical genre. Other scholars consign letters to a "pre-literary" status (Frühwald, Mähl, and Müller-Seidel). On the one hand, the personal letters of some critically acclaimed authors have served as a valuable but limited arena to rehearse specific aspects of writing destined for subsequent fictional publications. On the other hand, these three letter writers manifest fully developed literary ambitions in their letters. The label pre-literary implies a lack of artistic sophistication that not only creates competition among literary genres but also marks diaries and letters as permanently subordinate to the accepted, canonical literary forms. If, as feminists point out, we need the chance to study women's art, history, and culture so as to begin to codify the patterns necessary to develop a substantial feminist aesthetic, and if — as Leslie Adelson argues — we are interested in designating a body of literature as "women's literature," apart from "men's literature," then we also need to remember and be wary of the pitfalls of separation (335–42). Separation may lead to being earmarked as inferior and perhaps being cut off like an incestuous clan.

An important distinction between correspondences and other literary genres is the problem of editorial selection and publication. Unlike most familiar literary works, correspondences are more like unfinished symphonies; they may have been published posthumously, may be incomplete, and are often without editorial oversight from the author. The decision of which particular letters to publish or even preserve has historically fallen to diverse individuals: editors, publishers, historians, scholars, surviving relatives, and — occasionally — the writers themselves. Letters are destroyed by correspondents wishing to preserve their privacy or are lost in wars and political upheavals. Unfortunately, published correspondences are usually not complete, and the decision when and where to break into segments the often enormous record is at times arbitrary. Especially in view of the potentially lifelong duration of letter writing, the sheer volume of a letter writer's production can bog down attempts to define a work of art that seems to be always still in progress. This problem takes on major proportions in the work of Schlegel-Schelling, who had no editorial control over the publication of her letters, and somewhat less so for Varnhagen, who gave some instructions to her husband for editing her letters and suggested posthumous publication. Editorial coherence is an entirely different kind of problem for

Arnim, who did edit her letters and Goethe's responses, quite intentionally, and in the process made many changes in the text of the original historical exchange. Arnim's letters may appear to be collected in a rather accidental, chronological order, but were in fact quite artfully arranged.

The more common problem, pertinent to Schlegel-Schelling's letters, is that the author never reviewed the letters, never decided which to include and which to omit, never decided if the letters should be arranged chronologically, thematically, or by correspondent. These decisions can often have a great effect on the apparent creative unity of the final work. The editors who make these decisions for the author do so sometimes wisely, sometimes not. Schlegel-Schelling's first editor censored and omitted letters referring to her illegitimate child, excising from the epistolary narrative the account of one of the subject's greatest personal tragedies. Later editors frequently abridged the correspondence. Since Schlegel-Schelling never intended to publish her letters, we can never know what final form the author might have given them. Most of the letters are not written for a general public, but for a specific, private acquaintance, and assume a knowledge of context which a reader of the published correspondence may not possess. This problem demands from the reader a kind of ingenuity that is usually not required when reading finished literary works. The reader must approach the order and contents of the text with an open mind. Not all the letters in the collection belong there. Many that do belong are absent. The reader will have questions that can no longer be answered from the surviving texts. The order of narrative sequences is not definitive. These problems increase the need to approach a correspondence as a work always in progress, one that presents as many possibilities as conclusions.

While most correspondences display this periodic extended narrative structure, it was particularly in the Romantic period that literary culture was open to the spontaneous, impulsive quality peculiar to personal letters. Historically, correspondence prospered during German Romanticism as a form particularly capable of expressing the period's cultural sensibilities. The Romantic fascination with letters was much influenced by Christian Gellert's 1751 publication on personal letter writing, *Briefe, nebst einer praktischen Abhandlung von dem guten Geschmack in Briefen*. Although it is not generally thought of as belonging to the Romantic period, many of its precepts anticipate the Romantic movement's rejection of rational order in favor of what Wordsworth in the Preface to *Lyrical Ballads* calls "the spontaneous overflow of powerful feelings." Gellert's essay takes the form of an instructional guide on personal letter writing. In contrast to the numerous handbooks on letter writing that came before it, it forbade objectivity, regularity, conventionality, and predictability from the personal letter. Gellert's declaration of epistolary independence had a broad influence. The young Goethe referred his sister to Gellert's *Letters, With a Practical Treatise* some twenty years after its publication. The letters of Schlegel-Schelling, Varnhagen, and Arnim all break with tradition and follow Gellert's precepts in that they too usually eschew the prescribed formulas for the letter salutation and close, tending more often toward an informality that late twentieth-century readers find familiar. Such informality and individuality lends itself well to a literature of intimacy and self-exploration.

Envisioning the Romantic period's proclivity for self-expression in epistolary form as a coherent genre is assisted by an important public manifestation of the form: the 1828 *Briefwechsel zwischen Schiller und Goethe*. Published in several volumes, the *Correspondence of Schiller and Goethe* was edited and published by Goethe himself, making him simultaneously an author external to the work and a literary figure within it. This book and its precedent-setting appearance challenged several women to put forth their artistic letters. Within a decade, both Arnim and Varnhagen had compiled or published similar epistolary works. The *Correspondence of Schiller and Goethe*, like the work of the three women, has for generations been treated by scholars as a historical document, a source of references to other publications by the two famous writers. Like the work of Schlegel-Schelling, Varnhagen, and Arnim, however, the Schiller-Goethe correspondence is an imaginative work in its own right, in which the two famous authors use the letter exchange as a means of self-discovery. At first, each sees in himself a conflict of opposites, then each becomes aware of a similar conflict in the other, and thus, through a specifically epistolary relationship, Schiller and Goethe are each able to construct a useful image of the self. In the correspondence, dialogue plays a fundamental role not repeated in subsequent epistolary publications. As letter writers, Schiller and Goethe use each other to see the self in a metaphoric mirror, a crucial aspect of all the major correspondences of the Romantic period.

In claiming that the correspondence form appealed to a uniquely Romantic sensibility, I do not wish to ignore the problematic issue of periodization. Whereas scholars such as Peter F. Waldeck are quite specific in discussing the qualities of the self of Storm-and-Stress writers, my study embraces a very broad understanding of Romanticism. I agree with Joel Porte who, in writing on the self in American Romanticism, defends his retention of the term Romanticism rather than denominating the historic years surveyed (10–16). Many feminists like Silvia Bovenschen resist the periodization of literature because it has traditionally excluded women writers whose works fail to fall neatly into traditional scholarly definitions of literary periodization ("Über die Frage" 60–75). In my view, the term German Romanticism refers to a tendency within literature in the late-eighteenth, early-nineteenth century. I retain the term as a heuristic device meant to indicate certain historical, cultural affinities between the authors, not to imply that they all consciously subscribed to some well-defined common philosophy. I furthermore hope that our understanding of the cultural complex of Romanticism will be enhanced and modified by the reconsideration of the epistolary and literary works of these three women.

The Epistolary Self — Elaborate, Episodic, and Creative

Correspondence provides us with a map of the obscure area at the interstice between the speaker's oral presentation of self and the narrator's recorded description of event, the point where recollection and utterance overlap. These very same texts can be read as autobiographical memoirs. However, unlike autobiography, which Spacks has termed the rhetoric of explanation (*Imagining* 313), the narrative atmosphere of correspondence relies on the strategies of persuasive discourse with a periodic, extended dimension; although letters are often derivative of oral traditions, the rhetoric of written discourse and the demands of extended communication clearly mark the genre of correspondence. Correspondences preserve — or perhaps trap — a self in progress. The term "self" refers here to what Stanley Corngold has defined as that aspect of the subject that is elaborated in literature or "the constitutive participation of the conscious subject" (1). None of these correspondences present to readers the factual self of an historic woman. The historic woman cannot be retrieved via the surviving texts. Just as biography can be used to illuminate fiction, but fiction cannot logically be read as providing incontrovertible evidence of biographical facts, so, too, must personal letters be treated cautiously. We wrong them and we diminish the accomplishments of the letter writers when we equate the texts of the letters with an objective chronicle.

By asserting that all three works used the genre of the literary correspondence to create an imaginative account of the self in progress, I ally myself with those, like Hans Ulrich Gumbrecht who see genre theory as "keyed to literary history" and who "indicate a clear-cut sociohistorical interest in the literature of the past" (42). Genre functions more as a description of cultural phenomena than as a set of classical prescriptions. Moreover, the failure of correspondence to sustain itself beyond the Romantic period does not cast doubt on its status as a literary genre; genres are cultural phenomena to be identified by analysis of the extant texts. In the view of Genette, longevity of genres is not a certain proof of their transhistorical character ("Genres" 420–21). Such a working definition of correspondence as a description of certain epistolary and literary works begins with the concrete fact of publication; it may include both historical and fictional material.

Examination of the self has long been a staple of studies of German Romanticism. The self in the correspondence art of Schlegel-Schelling, Varnhagen, and Arnim is at times the familiar self of the privileged artist. In the introduction to her 1975 book on autobiography, Spacks discusses such aspects of writing the self, making it pertinent to the present study:

> To turn lives into words — whether those words claim to render fiction or fact — involves some act of the mind that discovers the logic of happenings in memory or imagination.... Putting a life into words rescues it from confusion, even when the words declare the omnipresence of confusion, since the act of declaring implies dominance. (*Imagining* 21)

Looking closely at the entire expanse of letters, it is possible to comprehend the author's concern with the developing and changing sense of self over the period of a lifetime. Moreover, it provides a discernible image of the moment of creation of a literary self — as Varnhagen puts it, an ego that has become an *I*. These literary selves are elaborate and episodic.

An in-depth study of the first of these women of letters is the work of the next chapter, which examines Schlegel-Schelling's life and epistolary self. Although her correspondence does not contain a narrative with an intricately geometric structure, as do many epistolary novels, it does manifest narrative patterning and chronological ordering. Schlegel-Schelling's correspondence is the least crafted of the three, the one that most closely resembles private, social letter writing. Her letters largely recount the events of her inner as well as her public life. She never edited her letters after sending them and never had any clear intention of publishing them. Yet even in as unedited a work as Schlegel-Schelling's, the reader encounters a complex and dramatic account of one woman's emerging, ever-changing epistolary self.

Then, the interpretation turns to the published works of Varnhagen and Arnim in the third and fourth chapters to demonstrate how letter writers of German Romanticism increasingly became epistolary authors, expanding their control over both the shape of the text and its entrance into public scrutiny as a published book. These two women use the personal letter as a means of self-expression and they use the genre of correspondence as a means of gaining self knowledge and thereby achieving self-vision. In terms of a descriptive genre study, Varnhagen's correspondence moves beyond Schlegel-Schelling's, because she collaborated with her husband in the shaping and arrangement of the book. Through the repetition and elaboration of the narratives of her letter writing, Varnhagen seeks to lend expression to a self in progress that can transcend lived experience and is free to speculate abstractly. Varnhagen's correspondence represents both a self in progress and a realized literary self.

The fourth chapter interprets *Goethe's Correspondence with a Child* as the act of Bettina von Arnim directly and dramatically creating a self that is capable of more conventional literary expression. Whereas the correspondences of Schlegel-Schelling and Varnhagen retain clear vestiges of historical letter writing and are books that preserve authentic cultural artifacts, Arnim sublimates the factual origins of the genre. Although based on an historical letter exchange with Goethe, the majority of the book is fictitious. Starting with letters written in the first decade of the nineteenth century, Arnim creates a work that permits a new self a full range of lyrical expression. She moves beyond even the descriptive definition and produces a work on the margins of correspondence.

Epistolary Narratives and Women's Artistic Aspirations

In sum, this study examines the writing of three women — Schlegel-Schelling, Varnhagen, and Arnim — as artistic self-expressions. All three works share in presenting a self entwined in literary production. The pages of these publications give rise to a literary self that evolves from the author's experiences, achievements, failures, utterances, contradictions, observations, style — in short, the growth of her person.

Far from being an informal and limited genre, the relative lack of prescribed convention for published correspondences gives letter writers freedom to innovate and to stretch the limits of self-expression. They make of the correspondence a genre with unique potential for expressing female creativity. For Varnhagen, the letter becomes a kind of ongoing philosophical essay. For Arnim, the letter evolves into a variety of poetic form. Rather than lamenting the limitations of the letter form, the reader never ceases to be impressed by the creativity and innovation with which these three women seek to transform and transcend those limitations.

2: Preserving the Self in Progress: Caroline Schlegel-Schelling

Although she repeatedly rejected roles she considered unfeminine, Caroline Schlegel-Schelling (1763–1809) never had the kind of conventional life lived by her mother or grandmother and envisioned for her as a girl. After being widowed in her twenties, she wanted to maintain the status of a single mother. When close friends became involved in the movement for German independence, Schlegel-Schelling was imprisoned by association. She married not once but three times — widowed by the first, divorced from the second, and then survived by her younger third husband. Her husbands, August Wilhelm Schlegel (1767–1845) and Friedrich Wilhelm Joseph Schelling (1775–1854), were prominent intellectuals and major figures in the German Romantic movement as well as being well acquainted with each other. She gave birth to four children: the three youngest died in childhood, while the oldest daughter, who had survived childhood illnesses and turmoil, then died of an infection as a teenager. All the domestic relationships that might have been simple and conventional in an another life were — for Schlegel-Schelling — fraught with conflict, crisis, and tragic outcomes. In looking at her biography in more detail, it is hard not to admire her perseverance while, at the same time, wondering why she seems so often to be on the verge of achievement when an extenuating circumstance strikes a blow against her. Potential, conflict, and tragedy are the recurrent terms in describing the events of her life.

Born Dorothea Caroline Albertine Michaelis in Göttingen on September 2, 1763, she was the daughter of an established and well-respected professor at the university. In English, her life has been sketched by Sara Friedrichsmeyer ("Caroline") and Janice Murray, and is described in a dated, but full-length study by Cecily Sidgwick written in 1889. There are also German biographies by Eckart Kleßmann and Gisela F. Ritchie. Her father, Johann David Michaelis, was a theologian and orientalist who devoted himself to his studies and filled the home with books. Schlegel-Schelling's parents permitted their daughters as well as their sons to participate in lively intellectual discussions with the university students and with distinguished visitors who included Lessing, Lichtenberg, and Goethe. Schlegel-Schelling's education, while received at home, was exceptional. She studied and spoke French, wrote letters, read, and debated works of the Enlightenment, and developed an appetite for contemporary literature. She wanted to be able to discuss, debate, and appreciate these works in conversations in her parents' home with professors and writers and to have her independence and accuracy of judgment acknowledged and admired.

Her education was nevertheless limited because she was denied the systematic university study her brothers received. She was never permitted to study mathematics, science, or Classical languages and literatures, prerequisites to a contemporary formal education. Despite the general view of Göttingen's educators that Schlegel-Schelling's powers of perception and intelligence were exceptional, neither she nor her parents aspired to anything more than a conventional, genteel marriage for her. Among her acquaintances was one woman, Dorothea Schlözer, who earned a doctorate under her father's tutelage. Schlegel-Schelling was critical of Schlözer, seeing her as an oddity, an unnaturally intellectual woman who displayed inappropriate brilliance in an arena rightly predominated by men. And, despite Schlegel-Schelling's eloquent praise of intellectual independence and keen perception of literary beauty, she did not aspire to be a published writer herself. For Schlegel-Schelling, to have done so would have meant fighting against all odds. Yet her upbringing in Göttingen indulged her with liberal intellectual privileges that she valued her entire life and made it difficult for her to accept the underprivileged feminine role normally assigned to women even though she wished ardently to fulfill this role and to do it well.

She was married on June 15, 1784 to Johann Franz Wilhelm Böhmer, a solid acquaintance of her brother, the son of one of her father's colleagues at the university of Göttingen and a physician, making his home and practice in the sparsely populated town of Clausthal in the Harz mountain region. Schlegel-Schelling was twenty-one and pleased to submit to the choice made for her and approved by her family.

While the published letters include some youthful writings, the bulk of the letters date from the twenty-four years following her first marriage. In the earliest letters after her marriage to Böhmer, she takes pains to show that she evaluates her deeds and ideas according to her own standards rather than unquestioningly adopting her parents' judgments. Yet, she does not feel her interests in conflict with theirs. In describing her wedding day to her friends Gotter and Bertuch, she mentions her parents calmly and analytically, even while relating her feelings of elation.

> If I only had you here with me, and if, instead of this tiresome writing, which loses so much, I could describe it to you in person. I don't know how I am supposed to lead you both through 4 such weeks with my pen. Spare me, at least, the story of my emotions; what they were, you can devise from the events, and how — I cannot describe it. What a whirl of love, friendship, and happiness I have experienced, and with such sweet melancholy — always on the border where pain and joy meet . . . . At the table I

> had my hair done, Friederike and Lotte tied the bridal wreath of real myrtle in my hair. Then I spoke with my father and got dressed.... The room was lovingly decorated by my mother's own hands.
> (To Gotter and Bertuch, 9 July 1784; 1: 92–93)

Her marriage to Böhmer particularly pleased her brother: "My brother is giving me to the man whom he destined for me since my childhood, to his best friend, who has loved me since that time.... Guided by these powerful reasons, I have made my choice" (To Studnitz, 17 Feb. 1784; 1: 77). Compare her letter quoted above with letters by her peers, who acutely felt the immaturity or impossibility of being married. Henriette Herz (1764–1847) was extremely young when her husband was chosen for her.

> I was perhaps twelve years old.... I might have been going to sewing school for about six months, when mother told me that I was to go back to my aunt for sewing lessons, and indeed wasn't I surprised, when she told me in confidence that I was to be married — with whom? I asked her, and she named the man; he was a prospective practical doctor, I had seen him a few times at my father's and certainly also in his window.... I was happy as a child about becoming a bride.... at the noon meal my father asked me. And I answered that I was satisfied with everything he would decide for me. (Herz 21–22)

Therese Heyne Forster-Huber (1764–1829) continues narrating this scenario where Henriette Herz leaves off:

> ... when I married, I was more innocent than a child. It was four weeks after the wedding until I became a woman, because nature had not destined us to be man and wife. I cried in his arms and cursed nature who had turned this agony into ecstasy — finally, I became accustomed to it....
> (To Schlegel-Schelling; 1: 325)

Although the young Schlegel-Schelling prefaces her wedding narrative with a cliché about writing — "If only I could tell you!" — she manages above and throughout her voluminous correspondence to recount an inner monologue to her peers simultaneously as she narrates the events of the recent past.

Clausthal was, for the eighteenth-century traveler, a considerable journey from Göttingen; it was remote and provincial. While critics still disagree about the felicity of the first marriage, young Böhmer died before they were married even four years. Schlegel-Schelling had given birth to two girls and was pregnant with third child at the time. Shortly after the death of her husband, she gave birth to a boy, Wilhelm, but he died within weeks. Schlegel-Schelling had left Clausthal and returned to Göttingen, where she had her daughters and a widow's pension, but no home of her own. She visited her friends the Gotters in Gotha for an extended stay and tried to keep house for her brother in Marburg. In the years after Böhmer's death, she moved often, establishing a pattern she was to follow the rest of her life. She felt deeply the next tragic blow, the death of her younger daughter. Therese Böhmer, known as Rose, died before her second birthday. Thus, in 1790 at the age of twenty-six, Caroline Schlegel-Schelling was a widow with one young daughter, having lost a husband and two babies.

The small family headed by an independently minded single mother moved to the city of Mainz. There, Schlegel-Schelling had a close friend from her girlhood, Therese Forster-Huber née Heyne (1764–1829), who was then in her first marriage to Georg Forster (1754–1794). Georg Forster, famous for having voyaged with Captain Cook, moved to Mainz when given the position of university librarian. Soon, he gained notoriety for his support of political changes influenced by French Revolutionary theorists. To Schlegel-Schelling, Mainz was an escape from the provinciality of Clausthal. No longer in mourning for her husband or infant son, she made friends and enjoyed the faster pace of her new life and the return to the intellectual atmosphere of a professor's home. Mainz turned out to be a historically significant place to be in those years. When French troops occupied the city, Forster became a leading figure in the short-lived Mainz republic.

After the fact, Schlegel-Schelling denied being involved directly with politics, yet she was a sympathizer of Forster's and by association must have endorsed many of his revolutionary ideas. Her letters, even before the French retreat from Mainz, show that she saw her role as a feminine one; although she used her own intelligence to evaluate the political ideas being discussed in the household, she never became actively involved. She did attend meetings of the Jacobin Club, listened to German and French republicans, and put the losses of Clausthal and Göttingen and Marburg behind her. When the French army officers of good breeding and taste were in Mainz, she participated in social events with them. And it was at that time that one of the assistant officers, Jean-Baptiste Dubois-Crancé (1773–1800), became her lover. The extant letters tell us almost nothing directly about her relationship to Crancé. Biographers do know that Schlegel-Schelling became pregnant with Crancé's child.

The political innovations of Mainz, however, were short-lived and proved nearly disastrous for Schlegel-Schelling. Not only was her friend Georg Forster discredited and labeled an opponent of the German government; she was as well. In March of 1793, she and her young daughter Auguste left Mainz to visit family friends. Instead of reaching Gotha, they were brought on April 8, 1793 to a Prussian military installation in the fortress in Königstein im Taunus. While she repeatedly averred innocence of political wrongdoing, her brother-in-law George Böhmer had acted as an assistant to the French general, Custine, who had taken over Mainz.

Schlegel-Schelling wrote letters to family, friends, influential acquaintances, and powerful noblemen to procure release for herself and her daughter. To the Prussian troops, both fraternization with the revolutionary French and sympathy with their democratic ideals might have seemed traitorous enough to extend her detention.

It was crucial to hide her pregnancy, for she feared she would be tried for treason and would lose custody of her first daughter if the illegitimate pregnancy were discovered. She saw an urgent need to be released from captivity. From this period, most of her letters have been destroyed; nevertheless, from later letters written by, among others, Therese Huber, Forster's ex-wife, we know that Schlegel-Schelling had obtained poison and was resolved to take it if her release became impossible.

Fortunately, her release did come on the eleventh of July; when she was about six months pregnant. Her brother Philipp procured official release documents from the king of Prussia, while her friend and admirer August Wilhelm Schlegel personally accompanied her to Leipzig and arranged for his younger brother and a colleague to continue to care for her in the small town of Lucka. There, under the assumed name of Julie Krantz, she gave birth to a boy, Wilhelm Julius Krantz, on November 4, 1793, and left him after about three months in the care of foster parents. She seems to have hoped to return for him. The child's father sent an offer of marriage and financial support; Schlegel-Schelling declined the marriage but accepted the support. Unfortunately, the baby also died prematurely in April 1795, passing away sometime before his second birthday.

In 1796 she married her friend, the literary critic and Romantic theorist, August Wilhelm Schlegel. Together, they entertained and established a salon which became a meeting place where the members of the Schlegel circle discussed and formulated seminal Romantic ideals and philosophies. A common theme among early biographers is that the union with Schlegel was a loveless marriage of convenience. Even Huch, one of Schlegel-Schelling's early champions, felt compelled to excuse the second marriage (*Die Romantik* 1: 10). Given the difficulties facing single mothers in the period, her desire for a stable union with an exceptional man who was her friend and intellectual companion is understandable. Schlegel-Schelling was not a sentimentalist. Her disdain for effusive emotion is evident throughout her letters. She laughs at the emotional style of personal letters associated with Gleim, comments with sarcasm on the melodramatic aspects of the novels of Sophie von La Roche, and reports that the Schillerian image of domestic bliss in his "Glocke" inspires her to laughter (1: 189, 194).

> One has to admit that it seemed then that things weren't going to work out for some of our family, but in the end we are rather happy in the marriage department and praise God every day.

You wouldn't believe how indispensable I am to our friend Schlegel, and you'll take pleasure in our charming household.

It would be difficult to stay more than a day there. Schlegel would be far too alone. He has no one like me. (To Gotter, 1: 417, 424, and 432)

The Schlegels' home was busy and their literary efforts productive during their married life together in Jena, from 1796 to 1800. The household included her daughter Auguste, her husband, her brother-in-law, Friedrich Schlegel (1772–1829), her brother-in-law's mistress, Dorothea Mendelssohn Veit (1762–1839), and later Friedrich Wilhelm Joseph Schelling (1775–1854) as well as occasional visitors such as the Humboldts, the Schillers, and, occasionally, Goethe.

When Dorothea Veit arrived in Jena, she joined the household which Schlegel-Schelling governed. Dorothea Veit was the Jewish mistress of Friedrich Schlegel, the younger brother, and was still legally married to another man. The relationship between the two would-be sisters-in-law was awkward and unpleasant from the start. Nonetheless, Schlegel-Schelling managed the literary productivity and the societal collectivity of the large household through a prodigious effort, initially with great success. The Schlegels translated no fewer than six Shakespeare plays in the years between 1797 and 1799, including *Romeo and Juliet*, *Hamlet*, and *The Tempest*.

But Schlegel-Schelling's life never went for long stretches without tragedy, and the Jena Circle of Romantics soon dissolved. The unpleasantness between Caroline Schlegel and Dorothea Veit Schlegel (she married Friedrich in 1803) grew to discord between the couples. It was in this period that Schlegel-Schelling developed a strong and almost painful attraction, a complicated love for the philosophically-minded physician, Friedrich Wilhelm Joseph Schelling, twelve years her junior. She felt a strong attachment to Schelling but recognized that he was perhaps too young for her. She wanted to foster the religious philosopher in him, yet she was not clear what role she should play, and she gradually progressed from friend and mentor to become his lover. These events are only described obliquely in the surviving letters.

And then in 1801, tragedy struck. Auguste Böhmer, Schlegel-Schelling's first-born, only- surviving child, died at the age of fifteen, probably of dysentery. Schlegel-Schelling was stricken with debilitating grief. The guilt that compounded her grief was made complex by the fact that when Schlegel-Schelling had the same illness, she recovered. Schelling, who had studied medicine, was involved in her cure.

Schlegel-Schelling was devastated. She seems in retrospect to have viewed her marriage to August Wilhelm Schlegel as centered around raising her daughter. With the death of her daughter, she was no longer able to find happiness or stability in her marriage. Schlegel was also hurt deeply by the loss of his stepchild. Schlegel-Schelling and her husband stopped trying to maintain their marriage, and she and Joseph Schelling openly acknowledged their romantic attachment.

In the year 1803, she and August Wilhelm Schlegel were divorced on May 17. Surprisingly, she and Schlegel remained on good terms when they parted. She and Friedrich Wilhelm Joseph Schelling were married on June 26. Her first marriage had lasted about four years until her husband died; her second lasted not much longer, about five years; and her third and last marriage was not destined to endure much longer. She retired from the public role she had played in Jena at the center of a literary community and devoted her energies entirely to supporting her husband's career in academia, moving first to the university in Würzburg and then eventually Munich, where she and Schelling received August Wilhelm Schlegel with his traveling companion Madame de Staël in 1807. It was also in Munich that she met Bettina von Arnim; Schlegel-Schelling found the young Arnim excessive and contrived. The difference in their ages prevented any deeper relationship. Finally, a little more than five years after having married Schelling, she contracted an illness that turned out to be fatal. Schlegel-Schelling died in 1809, in her mid-forties.

One of her legacies was the salon she and Schlegel sponsored and the atmosphere of collectivity in which they formulated the seminal doctrines of the Romantic movement; another is her contribution to her husband's translations and other literary work. However, her lasting achievements are her letters.

Caroline: Briefe aus der Frühromantik

Caroline Schlegel-Schelling's letters are the most subtle of the three addressed in this study. They are the ones that most obviously derive from a woman's social correspondence. Although she published a few anonymous reviews and collaborated on her second husband's translations, she declined to seek publication for her life's work — her letters. Her letters were privately circulated at times among a sizable community of contemporaries but were not published until 1871, by Schelling's son-in-law, Georg Waitz, long after she and her contemporaries had passed away. They are the most intimate of the three correspondences, but also the ones most concerned with everyday life. At the same time, Schlegel-Schelling's letters are not merely social documents. Although they give a vivid account of a German life at the time of the French Revolution and the cultural revolutions championed by her influential husbands, Schlegel and Schelling, those revolutions are not the central concern of Schlegel-Schelling's writing — rather it is her private life about which she cares most passionately. She is a careful artist whose letters portray an active intelligence reacting and adapting to the complicated circumstances of her life. Like leitmotifs in a symphony, imagination, friendship, tragedy, and relentless introspection give the correspondence continuity and coherence. The motifs surface, submerge, and resurface throughout the correspondence. Throughout it all, Schlegel-Schelling's correspondence dramatizes a critical temperament, an intelligence, the difficult and ever-changing process that is the lived development of a female self.

In her correspondence, Schlegel-Schelling holds up a mirror in an effort to reflect her written image. The volume of letters captures within a prose narrative frame the female self in the process of development. She strives as a letter writer neither to beautify nor to vilify nor in any way alter the self but to represent her self honestly and insightfully. The events of Schlegel-Schelling's life were tragic and dramatic. Surprisingly, in contrast to her biography, the letters are not filled with high drama and passion. On the contrary, Schlegel-Schelling's dominant emotion is restraint. Her letters portray an ongoing effort to bring order and tranquillity to a life that often lacked those qualities.

To Caroline Schlegel-Schelling the very notion that her letters could reach an extended public was almost unthinkable. Her reluctance to see herself as a public artist — so unlike the attitudes of Varnhagen, and Arnim — contributes to several major differences between her work and theirs. Perhaps most obviously, although an arduous and skilled letter writer, she did not, like Arnim, edit her own letters. For this reason, editorial coherence is a problem in her correspondence demanding critical attention in a way that it is not in the other correspondences.

The difference in social status leads to crucial thematic differences between her letters and those of her male contemporaries. Most of the canonical male letter-writers of the period, like Goethe and Schiller, write about themselves as artists, and use their letters to debate public, philosophical questions of aesthetics. Schlegel-Schelling shies away from so public a discourse, occasionally addressing similar questions but only among discussions of personal and domestic affairs. Her letters depict her intellectual life, yet this life cannot be separated without the Woolfian difficulty of defining the feminine from the complicated events in her personal life: her family, her need for social interaction, her relationships with her husbands, her private friendships — her role as salonière, wife, mother, and lover. Her letter writing can and should be read as a work of imaginative literature in which she struggles to express and to reconcile the various identities that she adopts in the course of her life.

This chapter will consider in sequence the major problems of Schlegel-Schelling's correspondence — most, it will be seen, unique to her role as a woman writing letters in the Romantic period. The first section considers how the problems of gender and genre play out in Schlegel-Schelling's work, exploring how being a woman both constrained and vitalized her letter writing. Section two considers how the author's failure to edit her letters for publication, an intentional but nonetheless problematic failure, makes the coherence and unity of the correspondence a challenge in a way that it is not for the other epistolary authors. Finally, looking more closely at the entire expanse of the letters, section three attempts to show how the correspondence is dominated by the author's concern with the presentation of the female self over the period of a lifetime.

Schlegel-Schelling and Genre:
Private and Public Personal Letters

> All at once in their midst, placed before strange scenery and into an entirely different circle of people and torn away from my own. — Yes, this is a big step. I could not take it, if I did not have unlimited trust in the man for whose benefit I do it, and if I were not submitting to him completely persuaded that he will do everything in his power to sweeten things for me.
> (To Gotter and Bertuch, 28 May 1784; *CS* 1: 89)

To Schlegel-Schelling and her contemporaries, the notion of personal narrative was familiar even if the term was not part of ordinary discourse. Schlegel-Schelling's circle were comfortable reading non-fictional works of privacy and open-endedness, such as the letter, memoir, and diary; and they knew how to set aside expectations of imaginative plot and definitive closure. The standards against which such writing should be measured do not derive from the conventional canon of poetry, drama, and novels. The development of a multi-faceted, cogent, and meditative self provides a thematic focus. In Varnhagen and Arnim, other literary forms are intermixed with the personal letter: Varnhagen's book begins with a memoir while Arnim's concludes with a diary. In Schlegel-Schelling's work, the narrative consists entirely of letters.

Altman analyzes the form of epistolary fiction lucidly, observing that "discontinuity is built into the very blank space that makes of each letter a footprint rather than a path. Yet as any observer of perceptual behavior knows, the illusion of a continuous line can be produced from a series of points" (169). She lists four rules for authors who wish to maximize continuity:

1. A single plot; 2. Linear time followed in strict chronological order; 3. One writer, one addressee; 4. Intervals between letters either not emphasized or filled in by what the letters report. (169)

Schlegel-Schelling, not writing fiction, breaks rules one, three, and four. She employs technique two; yet it is her editor who set her letters in chronological order. Thus, the formal criteria in fictional epistolarity, while related, clearly diverge from those of non-fictional epistolarity. Viewed as an autobiography, *Caroline* also fails Altman's four rules to maximize discontinuity, particularly since the intervals between the letters do not contribute to the narrative of her life (170–71). Furthermore, the illusions of narrative continuity and discontinuity are not played off one another.

Even though Schlegel-Schelling did not leave memoirs or diaries, she was a critical reader of such personal narratives. She reads Friederike Brun-Münter's diary with literary standards of personal writing in mind and does not hesitate to criticize the diary as poorly written:

> I cannot say that the rest of her diary was enjoyable. It seems to me that there are so many repetitions and so many words to which she hardly ever joins sense because she did not make and think herself, but rather took them from poets whose works seem to float so freely in her memory that she has confused herself with them. She has worked herself into a poetic frenzy, nothing is more easily forgiven especially because she is so young, but she must become gentler, her heart more consistent and her understanding sharper. First, then, would be the kind of softness that easily degenerates into sentimentality, and the second would be to lose her peculiarity. She seems to me to have more skill than understanding, if by understanding I mean seeing people and things in to their genuine (unpoetic) perspective. (To Gotter, 6 Feb. 1783; *CS* 1: 70)

Schlegel-Schelling does not treat Brun-Münter's diary as a factual autobiography but rather as a literary personal narrative, albeit a flawed one that does not meet her high expectations. She is as thorough and exact in her aesthetic critique as she is in later passages in which she discusses well-known works such as Goethe's *Iphigenie* and Schiller's *Maria Stuart* and in her few reviews. Brun-Münter's diary functions as a negative model, while several other works, which Schlegel-Schelling requests by title — such as Montagu's letters — influence her style positively. Schlegel-Schelling applies an equally demanding aesthetic critique to her own writing, and consequently her letters better define a coherent self than Brun-Münter's.

That Schlegel-Schelling chose the personal letter as her primary genre does not mean that she chose to be obscure, ephemeral, or unknown to posterity. Nor does it mean that she writes "naturally" — if naturally means in ignorance of traditional standards (Kauffman 51; Goldsmith 47). Her punctuation is correct, varied, and temperate and her grammatical constructions clear, concise, and cogent. Although one key characteristic of the personal letter is its being written without the immediate or sole intent of publication, many letter writers do think of posterity, of increasing their reputation, and of perfecting their art. In Schlegel-Schelling's case, although she composes without any intent to generate income or publicity, she does not shy away from acknowledgment or artistry. Homans speaks of Dorothy Wordsworth's "resistance to poethood," which is "to assume what can never be finally verified, that she could have been a poet simply by choosing" (*Women* 41). In her Lacanian analysis of German women letter writers, Hahn asserts that women were encouraged to be readers and wives but were never — not even as letter writers — real authors. For her, an author must *sign his name*. In response, her notion relies on a valorized hierarchy of genre and "subscription to auctorial intent." Schlegel-Schelling's case is more complex than that of Dorothy Wordsworth or the situation suggested by Hahn; Becker-Cantarino views Schlegel-Schelling's case as typical of women Romantics who lived under gender censorship and were thus dependent on their husbands and male family members for a definition of literary authorship ("Gender" 88). Indeed, like Dorothy Wordsworth, Schlegel-Schelling shunned publication and restricted herself to private letter writing. However, although she refused to publish her entire correspondence, she was urged to print individual letters and actually did see several literary reviews to print, although anonymously or under a pen name, and collaborated extensively, although again anonymously, on her second husband's celebrated translation of Shakespeare. Furthermore, she circulated many more letters among acquaintances who included many of the major literary figures of the day. Although she chose never to publish under her name, she did seek acknowledgment for her literary artistry.

Schlegel-Schelling's own utterances on the topic explain the depth of her antipathy to publication: " . . . but in truth, I am just a good woman and not a heroine. I would give a piece of my life right now, if I could have avoided, at least in Germany, being torn out of the feminine sphere of anonymity" (To Gotter, 15 June 1793; *CS* 1: 293). Note the almost apologetic tone to literary critic Sigrid Weigel's remarks when citing this passage to demonstrate that German women writers refused to publish on the grounds that publication meant self-exposure:

> Thus, she resisted publishing her own works as an author, expressing herself instead in the private texts of letters; or she composed and edited texts that were then published under the name of her husband, A. W. Schlegel — and tried to search for independence, friendship, and love in the home. Even in this search she had — like so many women — to separate love and intellect. (Weigel 89–90)

Fear of exposure is the obvious reason why Schlegel-Schelling recalled letters from certain people and destroyed others. These conflicting desires for anonymity and yet acknowledged literary artistry may be hard for a modern reader to understand, but to Schlegel-Schelling they seemed quite normal. They reflect the complexity of her social position as a woman intellectual in the Romantic period who had to reconcile competing claims of marriage, domesticity, and social decorum, with her own literary talent and ambition.

The familiar letter was a viable, publishable form in Germany in the late eighteenth and nineteenth centuries, and, while Schlegel-Schelling chose not to publish under her name, there is no reason to doubt she could have done so, if she had wished. Other women, like Arnim's grandmother, Sophie von La Roche, were published authors in the period. In a personal letter to Schlegel-Schelling, her brother-in-law, the philosopher and writer, Friedrich Schlegel, suggested that she contribute to the journal *Lyceum* and — making no secret of his own agenda — that she write in one of two genres, reviews or letters.

> Don't let Wilhelm's pushing or your own shyness about work spoil the idea of making your own contributions. Yet if you can not or will not, then there is still much left for you — through engagement and advice, you can set right and double our enthusiasm.
>
> I always believed your natural form — and indeed I believe every person of power and intellect to have one — would be the rhapsody.... Do be careful in choosing a form, and take into consideration that you have thoroughly mastered the forms of the letter and the review. You will write some letters on Shakespeare's comic genius, won't you, if you approve of the suggestion? (To Schlegel-Schelling, Nov.? 1797; *CS* 1: 439–40)

Many men in the period had published letters, although, like Schiller's *Ästhetische Briefe über die Erziehung des Menschen* (1793–94), these published letters tended to be more essays in letter form than personal correspondences. Friedrich Schlegel's "On Philosophy: To Dorothea" and "Letter on the Novel" put forward philosophical arguments, like Schiller's, yet maintain qualities of the familiar letter. Georg Forster's "Letter Fragment to a German Writer, about Schiller's 'The Gods of Greece'" conjoins two of the more unusual forms, the letter and the fragment, to defend a lyric poem. Johann Georg Hamann's letter to Kraus, December 18, 1784, is yet another instance of a writer opting for the letter form — here, specifically the personal letter — to express public concerns (Hamann 5: 289–91 and Dotzler 341). In general, during the Romantic period, writers were fascinated with exploring new and unfamiliar literary forms and discovering their expressive possibilities. Friedrich Schlegel continued to encourage the publication of his wife's writing, going so far as to offer, if she herself declined, to publish it for her:

What could be published from your letters is too pure, beautiful, and tender for me to see it broken into fragments and made coquettish through the process of drawing excerpts. In contrast, I do think that it would not be impossible for me as a redactor to produce one magnificent, philosophic rhapsody out of your letters. (*CS* 1: 440)

Perhaps Schlegel-Schelling was hesitant to allow her brother-in-law to rewrite her letters. Friedrich Schlegel in his theoretical pronouncements on literature indicated his interest in the letter as a genre: "A dialog is a chain, or a garland of fragments. A correspondence is a dialog in expanded scale . . . " (*KFSA* 2: 176).

Schlegel-Schelling's conscientious abstention from publication may seem embarrassing when compared to Friedrich Schlegel's position on the role of women in society. In the terse aphorisms of the *Athenäum*, Schlegel diagnoses women's plight: "Women are treated as unfairly in poetry as in life" (*KFSA* 2: 170, No. 49). He ironically comments on socialized gender inequities: "Women will have to remain prudes as long as men are so emotional, dumb, and bad as to demand eternal innocence and a lack of education from them" (*KFSA* 2: 172, No. 31). Furthermore, in *Lucinde,* he boldly proposes that much could be gained if women were to behave like men. The passage occurs in "Dithyrambische Fantasie über die schönste Situation" (*KFSA* 5: 12–13). Schlegel's complex irony refers on one level to the sexual act of conception and procreation, to the literary act of textual creation on another, and also — on some more obscure level — to the public act of textual dissemination or publication. Schlegel-Schelling chose not to act like a man.

Schlegel-Schelling seemed to subscribe to a supposedly "natural" order that views publication as masculine. She hesitated to engage in masculine activity and the subsequent difficulty of returning to natural female privacy. Friedrich Schlegel echoes her sentiments and even her diction in a letter to his brother: "I wish she had always let men take care of public matters" (*Briefe* 145).

Schlegel-Schelling writes with a high degree of artistry. She controls her style almost to the point of obsession and crafts her correspondence; yet, because she agrees with male contemporaries who instruct women not to publish, she has little to say about the often adverse, often triumphant experience of other women letter writers who see their writing in print. When she did appear in print, it was either anonymously, or under her husband's name, as with her assistance with the translation of Shakespeare and the few book reviews she co-authored with Schelling or authored anonymously in her last years. The paradox, then, lies in the puzzling fact that although Schlegel-Schelling's letters are the least accessible with regard to interpreting the author's experience as a woman and writer, they present the most rigorous epistolary aesthetics in terms of style, structure, and organization (Nickisch, "Briefkultur" 406).

Schlegel-Schelling's epistolary writing presents the reader with a striking paradox. She writes to express herself, yet she claims not to want to reveal herself — that is her personal life — to public scrutiny. Moreover, she means her letters to be private, intimate expressions, yet she strives to conceal her most troubling experiences. This careful intimacy marks her correspondence with an unguarded authenticity rarely encountered in the more accessible and more familiar discourse of public literary works.

Schlegel-Schelling and Publication: Editorial Problematics

The final form of Schlegel-Schelling's text available to readers and critics has been and will always be the work of others; indeed, a series of partisan and sometimes unsympathetic editors has shaped the published correspondence. Readers may commonly think of the editor as playing a minor and subordinate role to the author, but in the case of Schlegel-Schelling, editors have attempted not merely to transmit her work but greatly influenced its reception through their choice of texts and focus on particular aspects of the letters to the exclusion of others. Listed outside of the main text on the book's title page, he or she has decided which supporting materials we readers have access to and has also controlled which primary texts can demand our attention. Her first editors set the tone for decades of criticism that focused on the scandalous nature of her romances, rather than considering the more literary qualities of the correspondence. The sheer volume of a correspondence and the inevitable selection and abridgment of that volume makes it impossible to ignore the role of the editor completely, even when one might wish to do so. So, before treating the correspondence as a literary work, we must map its editorial coherence.

Seven different editors have published editions of Schlegel-Schelling in the two hundred years since she wrote. Georg Waitz in 1871; Helene Stöcker in 1912; Erich Schmidt in 1913; Ernst Wieneke in 1914; Reinhard Buchwald in 1914; Willi A. Koch in 1951; and, most recently, Sigrid Damm in 1980. The editor plays a more significant role in preparing a collection of letters for publication than is usually the case with a novel, play, or any other work of art for which there is an established text. For example, Schlegel-Schelling's first editor, Waitz, chose to omit extant letters referring to her illegitimate child and the circumstances of her arrest on charges of sedition.

Four editions of Caroline Schlegel-Schelling's letters are noteworthy. Composed between 1778 and 1809, her letters first saw publication in 1871, when the historian, Georg Waitz, Schelling's son-in-law, edited, and published the bulk of the letters under the title: *Caroline: Briefe an ihre Geschwister, ihre Tochter Auguste, die Familie Gotter, F. L. W. Meyer, A. W. und Fr. Schlegel, J. Schelling u. a. nebst Briefen von A. W. und Fr. Schlegel u. a.* The subtitle lists the stages of personal experience: first the family into which she was born; then the family to which she was mother (she outlived even the one of her four children to survive childhood); next the friendships she made; and finally the famous men she lived and associated with. The volume also includes some of their letters. The single first name in Waitz's main title suggests familiarity and personality, and his introduction, notes, and selection underscore the biographical value of the letters. All subsequent publications, including the most recent one, derive from Waitz's original work.

The most complete and scholarly collection of her letters, appeared in 1913. Erich Schmidt, a Germanist, reproduced the text as Waitz transcribed it but significantly increased the size of the book while shortening the title: *Caroline: Briefe aus der Frühromantik* (Caroline: Letters of Early Romanticism). Like Waitz, Schmidt consulted Schlegel-Schelling's original letters in manuscript; fortunately the wording and punctuation of the individual letters are nearly identical in each edition, justifying subsequent editors' practice of relying on Schmidt (and through him Waitz) either for convenience or because letters have since been lost. The book, *Caroline: Briefe aus der Frühromantik*, totals 1, 510 pages in two volumes. The editor presents the main body of Schlegel-Schelling's letters chronologically and divides them into six sections labeled according to the locations where the letters were written; each section spans three or four years beginning in 1778 and ending in 1809.

Unintentionally, Schmidt's predecessor Waitz had encouraged censorious critics. Waitz left gaps in Schlegel-Schelling's correspondence, hoping to avoid controversy. Subsequent critics and readers, however, felt obliged to pass ethical judgment on what they deduced to be Schlegel-Schelling's morality (Gottschall 578). Waitz suppressed various letters because of what Schmidt terms "*Familienpietät*" (1: xx): Waitz was a son-in-law of Schlegel-Schelling's last husband. The most contentious letters concern Schlegel-Schelling's political activities under the radical government of the Mainz Republic and the illegitimate birth of her fourth child, which Schmidt terms "the crisis of Lucka." Schmidt's unexpurgated version partially put an end to calumnious speculation, despite the continued absence (probably due to destruction) of many letters. Among the missing are letters to her acquaintance Georg Tatter, the Schlegels, and those written to her sister, Luise

Wiedemann. These last were probably destroyed by Schlegel-Schelling. Contemporary to the publication, the fascination of reviewers with the scandalous aspects of her life precluded a genuinely critical evaluation of the book.

Before considering the Schmidt edition of 1913, which is the most complete scholarly edition, mention should be made of two subsequent editions which were important in the reception history of the correspondence. It was Buchwald's edition of 1914, the sixth edition chronologically, that more or less put an end to the venomous debate over Schlegel-Schelling's morality and set the stage for serious scholarly study of her work (Stöcker; Huch; Damm). Immediately following Schmidt's 1913 edition, Reinhard Buchwald, who had assisted Schmidt, culled about one-third of the available letters and enlisted Huch, a novelist and scholar, to write the introduction. In 1899 in her *Blütezeit der Romantik*, she had included a chapter on Schlegel-Schelling, and, in her introduction to Buchwald's 1914 edition, she absolves Schlegel-Schelling on the one hand from wrong-doing for conceiving a child with Crancé to whom she was not married and, on the other hand, faults her for falling in love with men who were less intelligent than she, with whom she had no "inner affinity" (*Die Romantik* 1: 35, 39). Recent biographical sketches echo Huch's judgment, indicating that Schlegel-Schelling's life story continues to intrigue critics (Dischner; Stern 8–19; Panke-Kochinke 105–07).

Buchwald's *Carolinens Leben* is a clear precursor to the most recent edition, put out by Sigrid Damm. This edition was part of a renaissance in the 1980s of study of German women Romantics. In this vein Damm edited and introduced a volume in 1980, which is available in paperback. Damm gave her volume the somewhat cumbersome title, *Caroline Schlegel-Schelling: "Lieber Freund, ich komme weit her schon an diesem frühen Morgen": Briefe*.

Returning to the Schmidt edition, it is not the relative lack of abridgement that distinguishes it from the others, including the two more recent ones; Schmidt's book is in fact abridged, because, even though his principles of selection were not moralistic, he did delete passages he thought lacked interest. Just as an example, he leaves out materials such as lists of books she requested from various correspondents while in Clausthal, where she had difficulty buying books. While Schmidt judged these lists to be marginal to the correspondence, a reader interested in her intellectual development might disagree. While most must content themselves with reading the published editions, the ideal reader would supplement the Schmidt edition with deleted passages from various sources as well as the records of her intimates, the Schlegels and others. Schmidt's edition is nevertheless important because it promotes an interpretation of the correspondence as a literary work and attempts to clarify without being intrusive.

In the supplementary materials, the Schmidt edition introduces Schlegel-Schelling's correspondence as an exemplary literary work of Romanticism. He views the correspondence as one of three major works that narrate the history of literary Romanticism, the others being Wilhelm Dilthey's *Leben Schleiermachers* and Haym's *Die romantische Schule* (1: v). He requests, moreover, an objective, critical reading: "Our new edition ... knows no such politics; along with evidence of love and admiration, it allows a certain amount of antipathy to come to the fore, it exercises no advocacy pro or con, because this unique woman is strong enough to stand on her own" (1: xx). Schmidt's eighty-year-old challenge asks the reader to permit Schlegel-Schelling to define herself.

In providing context, the editor can have an enormous influence on the reader's perception of the epistolary narrative. Let us take as an example Schlegel-Schelling's involvement with the political revolutionary, Georg Forster. The extant letters fail to narrate her relationship to him comprehensively. Reading all her letters written from or alluding to the Forsters' residence fails to determine decisively the extent of her involvement with Forster and his radical politics. Within the correspondence, Schlegel-Schelling is discreet about the facts. It becomes helpful to flip to the notes for biographical information — information garnered from third-party letters and outside documents. Text and notes confirm that she had participated in topical political discussions under Forster's influence but had never actively campaigned for the independence of the short-lived Mainz Republic. Without contextual information, the following passage would be obscure:

> As for my guilt or innocence I can only tell you that since January, I've been deaf and dead towards any political interest — in the beginning I was heartily enthusiastic, and Forster's opinion of course pulled my own toward his — but I never proselytized either publicly or a privately . . . .
> (To Friedrich Meyer, 15 June 1793; *CS* 1: 297)

The passage taken only in the context of the correspondence would be cryptic. The reader needs to know that a misidentification of her late husband Böhmer (whose name she used at this time) and her friendship with the revolutionary, Forster, led the allied German forces to presume her guilty and take her and her daughter prisoner upon their departure from Mainz. Yet "guilt" here may allude to something else, something other than political wrongdoing. She was at the time pregnant with the child of the French officer, Jean Baptiste Dubois-Crancé. Although Crancé is of no importance to the published correspondence, the loss of Julius, their child, was a tragic event that enormously affected Schlegel-Schelling. Any reader wishing to make sense of her life must depend on the editor to fill in these gaps, and the skill and objectivity with which the editor performs this task cannot help but exert some influence on the experience of reading the letters.

Schlegel-Schelling's Personal Letters and the Construction of Self

Having reviewed the generic and editorial issues surrounding Schlegel-Schelling's letters, it is now possible to focus on a reading of the text in which she is more than a mere content provider. In this reading, she is like a literary composer, who constructs a symphony of self visionont of multiple epistolary entries, including discordant notes and contradictory explications. Therefore, two separate passages may both take up the same theme yet discuss it very differently. Indeed the four themes that recur throughout the letters to the extent that they can be termed leitmotifs are not factual descriptions of the friends she made or the tragic events that befell her. They appear instead as paragraphs of abstract musing on the nature of friendship, on the effects of mourning a tragedy, and on the role of the imagination and of introspection. The following four excerpts — all from one letter — concern the role of introspection and they exemplify how Schlegel-Schelling's letters foreground the textual ambition to construct an intellectual and epistolary self. It proceeds gradually, beginning with a perception of the need to organize concrete activities and abstract thoughts.

> It is always a woe for me when I am without a plan, whether in general or in specific, I won't so much as pick up a knitting needle unless I'm eager to complete the project and unless I have a overview of it and can afterwards think that I have actually accomplished something — that's when I can properly deliberate what I want to do . . . .
> (To Michaelis, 1786?; *CS* 1: 136–37)

Language does not prove inadequate in this letter; rather, it provides her with the means to articulate and then to overcome a lack of definition. In fact, it is not language that is incommensurate with experience but experience that fails to measure up to the act of writing. Shortly after the passage above, she continues:

> I wanted to write a letter — woe, woe, woe to those with such a desire; it was supposed to be out in the open, but my heart was an inhospitable island. There was the beginning of the letter, a thing to toss away, I can't write it, except in a delightful writer's frenzy, in which I then send out letters by the dozens. (To Michaelis, 1786?; *CS* 1: 137)

Although her heart may have been "an uninhabitable island" earlier, she populates this letter with thoughts on the nature of the human soul and discovers an entirely different geography of the self:

> Lotte, we would be miserable — if our happiness were not made up out of little concerns whose sum is vain, yet taken individually they are capable of thoroughly occupying us. For, out of the mood in which the soul seems to want to turn back upon itself and to be on the verge of fathoming its profundities and our very essence — out of this mood even the smallest thing can easily call us back, a voice, a fleeting glance that happens upon a book, or on some other thing — that can lead us like a flash back to the present, to comfort and the variety of life. Thus, discernment and joy come to life again. (To Michaelis, 1786?; *CS* 1: 138)

Schlegel-Schelling sees the abyss but does not fall; her writing acknowledges moments of silence but writes over them. Even though she does not achieve the total, unpoetic impartiality she seeks in her life, she approaches such a state in her letters. Finally, this letter turns to advice to her sister on how unmarried girls can be friends with married women. Curiously, perhaps, Schlegel-Schelling stresses the inequality among women:

> . . . see, it is and remains impossible for a woman to be like a girl. It makes a difference for the most distinguished creature to be a woman, only in another manner, how should it be otherwise for an ordinary one, for whom the goal of womanhood might well be the central human aim. (*CS* 1: 140)

The fact that the published editions only print Schlegel-Schelling's letters and omit most of the replies she received creates a strange generalizing effect in the correspondence. Although the letters were all written to specific acquaintances, the specificity of the addressee is lost to the modern reader. Although the *you*, in the form of "*Dir*" in the phrase, "because my letters always describe to you my entire soul," refers historically to Luise Stieler Gotter, we know little about Gotter, and naturally refer the letter to a generalized audience. Among the addressees of the correspondence, the *you* has many more referents, some were women and some men: Lotte Michaelis, Friedrich Meyer, and even the present readers. She writes to know what is happening in her self, for the recipient as well as for herself.

Schlegel-Schelling constructs in her letters from beginning to end a literary self in prose. Neither inaudible nor illegible, the epistolary self differs from both the protagonist of a first-person novel and the author of an autobiography. Altman, for one, points out that reciprocity is inherent in the epistolary experience but lacking in the autobiographical one and that "in the letter the past is always relative to the present" whereas in autobiography and memoirs "the present is subordinate to the past" (88–89; 123). While Jelinek straightforwardly eliminates letters from the genre of autobiography, a work written "with the intention of its being her life story" (xii), Domna C. Stanton's neologism "autogynography" might include *Caroline* as a work which dramatizes "the fundamental alterity and non-presence of the subject, even as it asserts itself discursively and strives toward an always impossible self-possession," (15) but only as a "usurper of male prerogatives" (13). The American writer Margaret Fuller's non-fictional epistolary writings and conversations, in which she uses conversation as a technique to "verify the mind's own voice" parallels Schlegel-Schelling's use of letter writing to construct what I term the prose self.

The strength and beauty of her letter writing derive from rich variety; its coherence lies in the integration and control of the constructed prose self. Reinhard M. G. Nickisch remarks on this aspect of Schlegel-Schelling's style when he observes that she uses:

> ... a language that is familiar with abbreviated syntax and that is lexically characterized by a natural and yet cultivatedly ordinary diction, in which the female writer remains always in closer proximity to the speech patterns of conversation than those of an essay. ("Briefkultur" 407)

Note that Nickisch places Schlegel-Schelling between two forms rather than evaluating her work under the rubric of letter writing. Some contemporaries expect a decentered or disintegrated self because they subscribe to deconstructionist beliefs about the self in letters. In Kauffman's words, "like the self, the language of the genre is fluid, decentered, multiple" (Kauffman, *Discourse* 32). However, I find that these terms do not entirely describe Schlegel-Schelling's prose self. In Schlegel-Schelling's text, we do not see the self becoming fragmented, losing its center, and multiplying. Instead, an uninterrupted reading has nearly the opposite effect. Each letter is indeed an installment distinct from the last, yet — when read serially — the prose text integrates the pieces and presents the mind with a self. Perhaps the best characterization of this literary self comes not from our own time but from one of Schlegel-Schelling's contemporaries, Samuel Taylor Coleridge.

> Now the Self is ever pre-supposed and like all other supersensual subjects can be made known to the Mind only by a representative: And again what that representative shall be is by no means unalterably fixed in human nature by nature itself; but on the contrary varies with the growth bodily, moral and intellectual of each individual. (Corngold 6)

French notes that Varnhagen, Sophie Mereau, and Karoline Günderrode use their letter writing to define a self, which is made unstable by the "failure of existing language to express female experience" (77) and thus "undermines any implications of authenticity" (74, 76, 86). Both the recent feminist view that all language is patriarchal and therefore incapable of expressing female experience (Cixous 253) and the post-structuralist view of language as incapable of representing the self (Derrida, "The Purveyor of Truth") prove insufficient in interpreting Schlegel-Schelling's relation to language and her letter writing. Corngold's drive to reaccredit the self of German Romanticism against attacks from French theory suggests the use of caution when reading eighteenth- and nineteenth-century texts through the lens of post-modern criticism. In the self-reflexivity of its content and the epistolarity of its form, Schlegel-Schelling's writing communicates the tragic story of the reintegration of her self. The reintegration, then, appears in a close reading.

Dated 4 September 1778, the first letter quotes from a short poem by Goethe, which initiates a thread of literary commentary on a variety of authors: Wieland, Schiller, Jean Paul, Moritz, Novalis, as well as Goethe. In 1778 at the age of fifteen, Schlegel-Schelling reproduces the dedication from Goethe's *Erwin und Elmire* as it appeared in a pirated edition.

> *Den kleinen Strauss, den ich Dir binde,*
> *Pflückt ich aus diesem Herzen hier,*
> *Nimm ihn gefällig an, Belinde,*
> *Den kleinen Strauss, er ist von mir.*

The small bouquet I made for you,
I plucked it from this heart, you see,
Take it freely, Belinda, do,
This small bouquet, it comes from me.

(To Gotter, 4 Sept. 1778; CS 1: 3; 672n)

An affirmative but critical reception of Goethe's oeuvre weaves throughout letters addressed to different recipients and provides thematic continuity. She offers Gotter and Bertuch her literary opinions well before her association with the writers of the Jena Circle of Romantics. She is proud of her early reception of Goethe's play *Iphigenie auf Tauris* (1787; *Iphigenia in Tauris*): "When he [Karl Wilhelm Thurneisen] heard, that I had Goethe's *Iphigenia* in manuscript, he was pleased to death..." (To Gotter and Bertuch, 28 May 1784; CS 1: 87). Although providing reception historians with a source for contemporary views of Goethe's writings, these views have a peculiar, empty ring when the letters are isolated from the entire correspondence of this writer who, despite a certain renown, is not known as an author (Rothmund; Kleßmann 296–97, 305; Jurgensen, *Das fiktionale Ich* 203.)

The four motifs however give her letters the coherence that justifies collecting them — despite the multiplicity of addressees — as one correspondence. They inspire a motivated reading and recognize Schlegel-

Schelling's participation in the generic discourse of correspondence. Schlegel-Schelling writes on literature with tremendous confidence; unconscious of the irony, she explores in letters to Studnitz and Gotter "what was happening in her heart" not confidently but tentatively:

> These past few days I haven't had any time for serious contemplation. What would the point be, since I believe I have already thought often enough. But it's unavoidable. Now my new unknown duties are lining up in front of me. All at once in their midst, placed before strange scenery and into an entirely different circle of people and torn away from my own. — Yes, this is big step. I could not take it, if I did not have unlimited trust in the man for whose benefit I do it, and if I were not submitting to him, completely persuaded that he will do everything in his power to sweeten things for me. O that none of his or my hopes are disappointed. I have been working on the plan to realize such hopes for some time now. May God help me to become the ideal that I see before my soul, so as to make us both happy and to make me worthier of my brother's love and of that of my ever dear friends. (To Gotter and Bertuch, 28 May 1784; *CS* 1: 89)

This early letter demonstrates her goal of making a whole by bringing all the parts of the self together. Knowing that Schlegel-Schelling married Böhmer on the advice of her brother introduces an intriguing ambiguity in the reading of the quoted passage: it is possible that the recipient of her unconditional trust, the man whom she wishes to please, and the one to whom she surrenders all authority with complete conviction is her brother, not her fiancé. It seems possible, that is, until the sentence in which she catalogs the exigencies necessary to realize her ideal self. With the help of God she will be happy with her husband, be loved and worthy of her brother; and be loved and worthy of her friends — God, her husband, then her brother, and last her friends. Although she mentions surrender, her diction counters that notion by repeatedly referring to her self. For example, she does not choose the stock phrase about "making him happy" but specifically includes herself: "to make us both happy."

The beginning of this prose self lies in the earliest letters in the correspondence from 1778 when she is fifteen. Schlegel-Schelling asserts that she knows herself even if her friends do not; the self is however under construction here. The subject who writes and speaks in the letters is still exploring herself, not yet achieving piercing self-examination. Schmidt's book represents these early years through letters to two female friends, Julie von Studnitz and, more extensively and more intimately, Luise Stieler Gotter. Schlegel-Schelling writes to Studnitz in French and states her awareness of the written medium: "Dear and tender friend, you don't know your Caroline very well if you can suspect her of not having been sincere in giving you the tribute that you deserve" (To von Studnitz, 28 Sept. 1778; *CS* 1: 4). A week later she puts it more explicitly: "Yes, my worthy Julie, no words can express what I feel. My heart has been penetrated with admiration and tenderness. I am hardly an enthusiast, I would never dare it, I simply tell you what is happening in my heart" (To Studnitz, 7 Oct. 1778; *CS* 1: 6).

The quotation below presents another self-conscious exploration in the written medium of the letter. Predictably, the date is also the same. The recipient here is Luise Gotter with whom Schlegel-Schelling corresponds in German.

> If I could only convey to you, my dearest and best friend, the emotions of my heart! But I can't, and why should I endeavor to do something, when I can see in advance, that I will never be able to find sufficient words to tell you all that my grateful heart feels for you. You consoled me with such mercy. No, Louise, I can never be entirely unhappy, because you are my friend. Believe it, I am not a sentimentalist or an enthusiast, my thoughts are the result of, if it is possible, cold-blooded contemplation.
> (To Gotter, 7 Oct. 1778; *CS* 1: 7)

Later in the letter quoted above, the fifteen-year-old Schlegel-Schelling points out to Gotter that her letters portray her entire soul. On one level, Schlegel-Schelling makes such a remark because it was fashionable; it was the mode of the friendship-cult enthusiasts like Christian Gellert — a cult to which she emphatically denied belonging.

> I have always claimed, and it remains true that I can live without love, but if you take friendship from me, you take away everything that makes life worth living for me. (To Gotter, 5 Oct. 1782; *CS* 1: 65)

> I wish I were there . . . to be able to thank you for your enduring friendship with tenderness and warmth, such as no pen can express, and where a glance, an embrace can say more than a thousand words. It is so sweet to be loved, and no heart feels it more, is more grateful and returns more love for love than mine. (To Gotter, 6 Feb. 1783; *CS* 1: 69)

On a more profound level than fashion, these remarks are prognostic and programmatic, for Schlegel-Schelling did go on to sculpt the image of her soul in her correspondence. Like Arnim and Varnhagen, Schlegel-Schelling writes a discourse expressing a deliberated subjectivity: both quotations above conclude by considering the self not the friend. Such subjectivity often proves more valuable to understanding a woman's existence than the most objective historical account. Ritchie endeavors to sort out the various predispositions of the biographers. She relies on a comparison between the biographer's version and an immanent study of Schlegel-Schelling's letters to dispel prejudices of male and female biographers. The term "subject" can mean both the topic of an account and the writer of such an account; in Schlegel-Schelling's correspondence, both senses of subject develop along a parallel course. Admittedly the events of her life had an important effect on her letter writing; however, it is not necessary to evaluate her life to interpret the correspondence. My argument differs from those who use the individual letters to construe the development of the self in a woman's life (Lüthi 56–8; Dischner, *Caroline*). Certainly, the events of her life should be used to illuminate a reading of the correspondence. It is similarly not surprising to find that Schlegel-Schelling's three marriages delineate the same pattern as does the literary development of the subject in her correspondence. Yet most biographers of Schlegel-Schelling record strikingly different judgments of her marriages. Her love for Schelling can be recounted as an aberration, the immoral seduction of a younger man by an older woman (Mielke 16–17). Recent critics such as Dischner, in "Die Romantikerin," praise her powerful female voice. In light of Schlegel-Schelling's own reticence about her marriages and her extensive epistolary deliberations about her self, moral biographies may fail to embrace the difficulty of the decisions she faced, and they are likely to overlook the complexity of her letter writing, the art of her correspondence.

Schlegel-Schelling challenges her friends to deduce her "sensitivities" ("*Empfindungen*") from the events, the events as Schlegel-Schelling perceives and recounts them. Thus, she explores and then overcomes the lack of immediacy in writing. The next letter dates from shortly after the Christmas holidays in provincial Clausthal, after she had lived there for a few years:

> It is peculiar that descriptions and representations make so very different an impression on us than the actual reality, of which we read a reflection, and that, with a painted world, one forgets oneself so easily and so willingly. Overall, nothing is so awful, nothing so pleasant as our power of imagination feels it is. For this reason, the soul is more desecrated through pictures that are a bit seductive and impure than through the deed, to give just one example among thousands, and I have often thought, that to be murdered could hardly be as terrible as the terrifying representation.
> (To Michaelis, 27 Dec. 1787; *CS* 1: 168–69)

Schlegel-Schelling recognizes that her writing, at this moment, could not adequately express her imagination and sensations. She puts the imagined experiences of a human subject into words and remarks on the discrepancy between the written result and the lived reality. She has a vivid picture in her mind of her own death — a drastic thought indeed. Yet she writes about the differences between reality and mimesis, ranking mimesis above reality and distanced reflection over immediate impression.

> I remain silent about my own happiness. Who wouldn't predict a description based on the first 6 weeks of matrimony? And yet I do believe that it will last, because it is not exaggerated. Böhmer has to be a good husband

as long as I love him, and my affection for him does not bear the stamp of explosive emotion. (To Gotter and Bertuch, 9 July 1784; *CS* 1: 97)

Schlegel-Schelling does not write here of a lack of love as many infer; instead, she literally writes that she prefers, for the time being, not to mention her happiness, because it is a symptom of being newlywed. To her sister, Schlegel-Schelling comments on the slowness and unevenness of the development of her self:

> My own burden oppresses me. It's always like this for me when I have gone too long without contemplating myself, and then I undergo a *révue*, there is much to be improved, and the worthy activity has become so slack, and one notices, if one is at least unbiased about oneself, that practically everything that makes us discontent is due to our own lack of the same. Hereafter it will be better — once more, one is better — then sinks again — and pulls oneself up again.
> (To Michaelis, 20 Mar. 1786; *CS* 1: 143–44)

The coherence of the correspondence rests not so much on biography as on tracing the development of the prose self. Neither purely self-reflective as it would be in an autobiography, nor cleverly reciprocal as in epistolary fiction, the self here disperses. It collapses into a collective subject: "*our* family" and "in the end, *we* are . . . ." It subordinates itself to the apostrophized *you* of both the addressee and the readers: "*You* won't believe" and "*you* will certainly have *your* joy in our household." Finally, neither totally invisible nor completely inaudible, it submerges under its own indirect object "to the friend." In the third quotation, Schlegel becomes the grammatical subject of the sentence and the first-person narrator his object: "He has no one like *me*."

In a sense, the biographical development of her third marriage parallels a change in the correspondence. Schelling was her husband from 1803 until her death on 7 September 1809. For the first time in her voluminous correspondence, passionate vocabulary surfaces in Schlegel-Schelling's letters, yet only in brief moments: "I love you so that I think it could cure you" (To Schelling, 6 Mar. 1801; *CS* 2: 70). These moments are indeed tender, yet they are not sustained or protracted but often reluctant.

> . . . my darling, whom I hold near my heart like a precious child and whom I respect like a man. You know I do both, and must sometimes reprimand you severely. My dear Joseph, do I look forward to seeing you? Yes indeed, my joy flies past the time that still separates us more that I can tell you.
> (To Schelling, Feb. 1801 [?]; *CS* 2: 73)

In the last nine years of her life, Schlegel-Schelling wrote many letters to Schelling, with whom, she states, she experienced the most grand and passionate love of her life. The letters, nevertheless, lack the vertigo, the intensity, the enthusiasm of the love letters Bettina von Arnim wrote, whether to Karoline Günderrode or Johann Wolfgang Goethe. Arnim first writes of the ecstasy of love in her twenties and sustains it well into her fifties, whereas the earliest extant love letter by Schlegel-Schelling stands at the end of a twenty-two-year long career of illustrious letters.

Her concern with constructing a literary self in her letters' prose reaches its first climax in letters written after the death of her first husband up to the death of her second child. She wishes to express her sorrow in a gentle manner yet finds this effort, countered by her grief, enormously difficult.

> To suffer gracefully is the greatest struggle, the most I am capable of, the most necessary, for eruptions of my troubles, unbridled tears of woe, instantly bring me pain. One profits greatly, when one suppresses them, one arrives at a dreamlike numbness. It's not as though I am trying to make myself have no feeling, or as if the pictures of the past were any less lively — your Caroline is a living monument to the departed one [her husband, Böhmer] — he lives in my heart in the most immediate of ways . . . .
> (To Gotter, 25 Oct. 1788; 1: 170)

Schlegel-Schelling's letters from the time of the death of her daughter Auguste are missing. After Böhmer's death in 1788, she moved several times, to stay with her mother in Göttingen and her brother in Marburg, before settling in Mainz with her friends the Forsters. "It is for the moment neither heaven nor hell, but Mainz, a place where people live, that is, a middling thing between the two" (1: 242). Her style is characterized by a rhythm of alternating short and long sentences; her word choice is precise and varied, filled with many French borrowings but not excessively so; also, she interspersus among the personal epistolary prose of this passage some general, objective comments narrated in the third person.

It is not, as Gellert and others would have it, the natural imitation of untrained conversation that makes the following letter describing the death of her twenty-month-old daughter so powerful. Instead, she maintains control of her style even when reporting the death of a child. Her control produces a hauntingly tragic tone:

> . . . in her quiet imaginings, she seemed to see something toward which she longingly reached out her beautiful arms, so that even her fingers seemed to be stretching. Then she grabbed me tightly by the hair — at one point she drew my hand firmly to her heart — with gentle convulsions, she plucked at the bed sheets — and I shut my eyes against this sign. During this time, she was entirely rational — she understood me when I spoke to her about Christmas gifts that Grandmother would send — and she was still able to answer — some for Gusten [the sister, Auguste], too.
> (To Philipp Michaelis? Dec. 1789; *CS* 1: 197)

Schlegel-Schelling describes the actual moment of the baby's death with understatement: "My Rose grew quiet . . . everything grew silent — and I wished ardently that nothing would ever break this silence" (*CS* 1: 198). Unlike the all-knowing reader, the letter writer does not know that the death of little Rose (Therese Böhmer) was to be an experience she had to relive with each of her children. Recall that Schlegel-Schelling bore four children yet lost all four of them. While three of them passed away before their second birthdays, the death of her oldest, Auguste Böhmer, was especially tragic. Not long after losing her Auguste, Schlegel-Schelling recounts the pain of watching another mother lose her child.

> My dear Wilhelm, I have suffered again a severe blow . . . . It was almost beyond my strength to be so reminded and to be there and see the pain. Yesterday morning it will be 8 days since I took the beautiful, sweet child from his mother and could not hold him in my arms, he was so lively. A half hour later he was brought screaming up to the room and only brought out again after falling into the sleep of death . . . . I went up and was inconsolable and ran back down to console him. O how much I missed you . . . . and the maid said that the child was looking at the picture; you remember that there is a small picture of Auguste hanging there . . . . Yes, he is now where she is, and during the night I pressed a kiss on his lips so that he can bring it to her.
> (To August Wilhelm Schlegel, 16 Mar. 1801; *CS* 2: 75–77)

An anti-climactic period of equally prodigious letter writing follows. In the 1790s Schlegel-Schelling's confidante and primary correspondent was not her husband, August Wilhelm Schlegel, but Friedrich Meyer (1759–1840), a prolific dramatist, a librarian in Göttingen, and a personal friend (*CS* 2: 672–73). Also, it is worth noting that Caroline Schlegel-Schelling corresponded with her friend, Georg Tatter, but their correspondence has been lost. Without these letters to include, it is not possible to derive a complete biography from the correspondence. Most of her letters to Meyer allude to shared intimate understanding despite the use of the formal pronoun:

> . . . the tone of your letter is a bit morose — but it is not my intention to convert you. I know too well that one does not do this in letters — I shall simply draw a cautionary lesson from your example. If I could see you — well — my cheerfulness would not intoxicate you — but one could still hope so. (To Meyer, 1791; *CS* 1: 241)

The years spent in Mainz between 1792 and 1793 offered Schlegel-Schelling an opportunity for tremendous independence and intellectual growth, yet they culminated in great adversity. In contrast to the restrained tone of the earlier sections, passages in some of these letters resemble excerpts from a historical novel in which Schlegel-Schelling is the narrator:

> We might still witness some very lively scenes if the war should break out — I wouldn't leave here on my life — just think, if I could tell my grandchildren stories about how I experienced a siege, saw an old clerical get his nose sliced off and the democrats grill it in the public market — we are indeed in a time of extremely interesting politics, and that gives me, in addition to the clever things I hear each evening during tea, an enormous amount to think about especially when I sit alone in my very pretty little room in the narrow little alley, sewing up scarves, as I am at this moment.
> (To Gotter, 20 Apr. 1792; *CS* 1: 250)

This is one of the most extended narratives of contemporary events in the correspondence. The author cleverly heightens the immediacy of such experienced history by juxtaposing various levels of history. She sets the mention of war, representing world-wide importance, next to an anecdote of localized reaction to world history, and concludes with a contrastingly peaceful depiction of her domestic existence — sewing scarves. The interposed statement, "I wouldn't leave here on my life," is meant to be figurative; yet it takes on an ominous meaning in light of the truly life-threatening outcome of her stay in Mainz. It is precisely yet ironically these life-threatening events of her sometimes exceptional and sometimes ordinary biography, vastly misrepresented and distorted by rumor, that make the developmental construction of self in the correspondence interesting to read.

Surprisingly, perhaps, reporting on political upheaval does not preoccupy the letter writer, who soon returns to her preferred topic: the state of her self, and especially the Romantic conflict between self and fate. The second climax of the tragic self occurs in two long letters to Meyer dated 16 March and 10 May 1794. Again, variation within individual letters adds to the drama of Schlegel-Schelling's prose.

> Read this when you are free of pain, for you will not be able to defend yourself against the new discomfort of the gout. At least, I believe it will be so — but perhaps in this, I ask too much of my heart. This much is certain, nothing is more inconvenient than to sympathize with me — and yet —
>
> > Though Fate may hate me still
> > Must you reiterate her pronouncements, too?
>
> [*mag mich noch so sehr das Schicksaal haßen,*
> *betest* Du *wohl seine Sprüche nach?*]
>
> Can you forgive me my unbounded misfortune? Indeed, Sir, you have far too sanguine a picture of my situation . . . .
> (To Meyer, 16 Mar. 1794; *CS* 1: 330)

In this relatively short excerpt, Caroline demands sympathy from the addressee, Meyer, with powerful authority. The next sentence immediately draws back from such authority; it interjects a touch of humility. Then she turns from the subject of Meyer's discomfort to a vast complaint of the lack of sympathy in the world, and she supports the observation with a quote from Meyer's own poetry, tailored to suit the situation and the self that records it. She exhausts the varieties of apostrophe by addressing the recipient with the informal, here intimate, *Du* (you). Finally, she returns to the polite address to establish the intentionality of her apostrophe. At the peak of its tragic development, Schlegel-Schelling's epistolary self culminates in an act of aggression.

The second tragic climax is not contained within one letter alone. It spills into a second, underscoring the ability of correspondence to capture the self in development. The second letter parallels the discourse of the first on a more playful and less pathetic level, and it also marks the change in her self-resolve. Here she combines three of her four favored motifs: she writes of literary productivity and merges friendly confidence with poignant introspection.

> Young Schlegel, who is also there now, you won't want to seek him out, will you? *It has always seemed to me that you have a thing against the Schlegels. As for me — I have a tender spot for them . . . . if I don't go to Dresden, I shall go to Holland — and this is quite decided . . . .* I am confessing to you in German and in French all that I have on my conscience — you are getting involved in a secret. Nothing less, you are a secret emissary — whom no one has sent and who goes to no one.
>
> (To Meyer, 7 June 1794; *CS* 1: 345; italicized sections in French)

Although biographers have depicted the third marriage to Schelling as the pinnacle of her biography, it does not represent the pinnacle of her correspondence. By the time she became acquainted with Schelling, her style had matured. She was at ease in the written medium of the letter yet had cultivated it as a means for expressing her self and not the self's attraction to another. Hence, she composed rather pedestrian love letters that interrupt themselves — "I can scarcely count the hours, until I hear your voice again and look into your eyes. Just now I have read Fichte's announcement. I can't deny, the passage has the finest ambiguity" (To Schelling, 1 Mar. 1801; *CS* 2: 57). Returning again to the biography for contextualization, her only child, her daughter Auguste, died at fifteen of dysentery the summer before, on 12 July 1800. Both mother and daughter became sick at the same time. Schlegel-Schelling had fought off at least two previous bouts of the same affliction — one incidence was cured by a controversial cure applied by none other than her future husband Schelling (Kleßmann 211–12). When Auguste contracted dysentery in 1800, Schelling again tried the same treatment, unsuccessfully. Although it is now impossible to know if Auguste Böhmer's death was avoidable, Schlegel-Schelling and her husband felt responsible. Schlegel-Schelling saw in her daughter her raison d'être. She confused her remorse about Auguste's death with her love for Schelling. Many former friends and colleagues — except, notably, August Wilhelm Schlegel — intensified the guilty feelings. Witness the confusion in this typical passage from one of Schlegel-Schelling's love letters:

> Take our peculiar relationship as it is . . . not as the purely mundane, beautiful, limited love of two beings, who encounter each other for the first time to exchange their freedom with each other, nor even a fearless breaking of all previous bonds, that love even in my situation could never count as a virtue. However, as much as it is — to our simple desires — too disjointed, it is everything in everything, I hold you to my breast as friend, as brother, as son and as beloved . . . .
> (To Schelling, Mar. 1801; *CS* 2: 60–61)

The ambivalence is unmistakable: "as friend, as brother, as son and as beloved." (Recall that our author was at this time still legally Caroline Schlegel and that Dorothea Schlegel was spreading calumnious rumors about her relationship with Schelling.)

Thus, while she writes to Schelling of the "fantastical" nature of their "alliance," she writes to Schlegel of the reality of the discrepancy: "Certainly I won't make a move without you . . . . What I have to tell you is simply this — I can never deny Schelling as my friend, but in no case can I trespass beyond a border we have agreed upon" (To Schlegel, 6 Mar. 1801; *CS* 2: 65). August Wilhelm Schlegel's actions were nothing if not chivalrous; he defended both Schelling and Schlegel-Schelling and was amicable about the divorce long afterward. Five years after their divorce, when Schlegel had become Madame de Staël's traveling companion, he spent a week with the Schellings. Schlegel-Schelling writes:

> We have seen Mrs. von Staël with her family and Schlegel here, just before Christmas. This visit, which lasted about 8 days, proved very pleasant for us. Schlegel was very healthy and cheerful, relationships were of the friendliest sort without any tension. (To Gotter, 15 Jan. 1808; *CS* 2: 514)

Love, for Schlegel-Schelling, need not reach the wild heights that it reaches in Arnim's letters. She met Arnim only once and quickly noticed her intelligence as well as her eccentricity.

> . . . then Bettine Brentano, who looks like a little Berlin Jew and stands on her head to be clever, not without intelligence, *to the contrary*, but it is awful that she is so confused and crazy and contrived; all the Brentanos are highly unnatural natures.
> (To Luise Wiedemann, Feb. 1809; *CS* 2: 541–42)

Schlegel-Schelling chooses the oxymoron "unnatural nature" to describe the young Arnim, at this time twenty years old. Schlegel-Schelling prefers to use the word "love" for less personal and less emotional objects than Arnim does. Viewing the same texts as a work of correspondence shows that the author Schlegel-Schelling often uses the word "love" impersonally and that she combines the idea of love with moderation and tolerance.

> [Tolerance] is to an extent the only way for me to participate here in the pleasures of the community, in part my love for seeing and hearing the fictional world is so great that I am pleased with very little.
> (To Gotter, Aug. 1805; *CS* 2: 412)

She wrote the above passage in Munich, associating love with collective undertakings instead of a single individual.

Perhaps it is because the collectivity in Jena ended so bitterly that Schlegel-Schelling here advocates tolerance so strongly. She continues the effort to implement Romantic ideals not only into the practice of writing on literature but also into ordinary existence. During the separation from Schlegel, Schlegel-Schelling describes to him the sort of joint activities she and Schelling engage in, stressing the intellectual, both between Schlegel and herself and between Schelling and herself.

> Because we must regularly be occupied with one another in order to stay in a routine, I only want to tell you, my dear Wilhelm, that Schelling is reading this file line for line with me, and it is beginning to become clear to me. It is a genuine pleasure to learn how to understand, and to brighten a dim image and finally to have the peace of the image itself.
> (To Schlegel, 18 May 1801; *CS* 2: 146)

On the one hand, the letter's recipient, Schlegel, receives information on an article by Fichte and maintains his relationship with the letter writer via this letter. As Schlegel-Schelling puts it: "we must regularly be occupied with one another." She characterizes the notion of mental comprehension in an appropriately impersonal voice. On the other hand, her use of a business tone ill fits the parallel she draws: falling in love.

The only sections in which Schlegel-Schelling abandons her "unpoetic" prose self in favor of the poetic beauty of a love lyric do not describe a male lover but rather abstract, philosophical topics. She hovers in a hazy plane among sentiments of love and religion and an analytical model of the secular world:

> Because the highest is not too high for — the very same little person who writes to you — therefore, I can comprehend this severe consequence, because it was explained to me in such a lively fashion, and this image of the world released from all that is subjective better than I could an image as clear as daylight. — And how peaceful that makes my heart. Yes, I believe in the heaven of Spinoza's soul, whose one and all must be the primary feeling, that is now pushing towards the light in Schelling.
> (To Schlegel, 18 May 1801; *CS* 2: 146–47)

Though Schlegel-Schelling was reluctant to become a public figure, her letters demonstrate that she was an insightful and talented artist. It is not possible in a simple way to summarize the complex process of reaction and adaptation that actually occurs in the letters. The correspondence can be read most productively as a series of reflections on the changing role of a woman's private life in a time of political and cultural tumult. Schlegel-Schelling grows to confront and survive the crises of political persecutions, illegitimacy, abandonment, the death of loved ones, and also new and mature loves. Through the course of the correspondence, we see the subject evolve, respond to circumstances, face and overcome adversity. And this evolution, this development of a female self is the central drama of the correspondence.

3: The Self from Ego to I: Rahel Levin Varnhagen

Rahel Levin Varnhagen's (1771–1833) successes include being one of Germany's leading intellectuals, presiding over popular and effective literary salons in two different decades, authoring a voluminous correspondence of ten thousand letters, and airing her views on contemporary literary criticism in six different publishing venues. At the same time, in the accounts of herself and her acquaintances, she was highly self-judgmental, manic, more than a little eccentric, and always battling against prejudice and a sense of inadequacy. Her letters are unique, a strange mixture of social insight and pessimism. While many letters describe her active social life in Berlin, her voracious reading habits, and her delight in friendships, there are others that wallow in isolation, that extol the uniqueness of her self, or that express her desire to escape social entanglements in order to enter a realm beyond, where philosophical speculation and spiritual sublimity dwell.

The exacting standards and high demands for achievement that she made on herself are magnified by her condition as a Jewish woman, an outsider in contemporary German society. Varnhagen entirely understood the multiple means others used to exclude her from the intellectual literary society she desired and helped create. These varied from blatant anti-Semitism, such as guests whom she received on her salon evenings who would not allow her as a Jew to enter their homes, to subtle forms of paternalistic sexism contained in references to her as "*die Kleine*" (the Little One). She dealt with her otherness differently at different times. Sometimes, she wrestled intellectually with the validity of societal constructs that define and empower insiders; she wished and strove other times to be accepted as an insider; she accepted periodically her extraordinariness with resignation; and at times she even celebrated her uniqueness.

An outsider as a Jew and a woman, she was also set apart from her peers by remaining an unmarried adult until age forty, by her family's wealth, and then by her poverty, which ensued from the wartime collapse of her father's business; she was set apart by her lack of a formal education and her innate intelligence. These inequities occupied Rahel Levin Varnhagen for most of her life. Even though she eventually married and became a Protestant, neither of these acts undid the earlier conditions of having been a Jew in a gentile world and a woman in a man's world.

Unfortunately, an up-to-date, book-length biography of Rahel Varnhagen is not available in English. Hannah Arendt's *Rahel Varnhagen*, most of which was written before the Second World War, offers an interpretation of Varnhagen's life as much as a historical biography; it was however first published in English and is available in a forthcoming new edition. Short sketches in English can be found in the *Dictionary of Literary Biography* and Blackwell and Zantop's *Bitter Healing*. In German, there are many sources; a comprehensive yet condensed biography can be found in Tewarson's *Rahel*.

Varnhagen's life fell half into the eighteenth century and half into the nineteenth. She was born in 1771 on May 19 to Chaie and Marcus Levin. Her father was very much a man of the eighteenth century. A prosperous jeweler and financial businessman, he was one of Berlin's few "protected Jews" (*Schutzjuden*) under Friedrich II (Tewarson, *Rahel* 11); as a result, her father had been granted more privileges than "unprotected" Jews for business and living, yet was neither without restrictions nor on equal footing with gentiles. Varnhagen was his oldest child, born when he was already forty-eight years old. He adored his exceptionally intelligent daughter, yet he dominated her as he did the rest of his family. Varnhagen saw her role in family life as an intermediary who protected her younger brothers, sister, and even mother whenever possible from the arbitrary authority of her father. She repeatedly levies sharp criticism against her education, calling herself an ignoramus, bemoaning that she was never taught anything, and had no formal training or studies. In spite of the perceived inadequacies of her education, she was extraordinarily cultured and literate. Her music lessons brought her the study of the piano, the violin, and composition. She was especially well-read in the philosophers and poets of the Enlightenment and her own age: Lessing, Ramler, Nicolai, Mendelssohn, Jacobi, Humboldt, and Fichte. Under her own initiative, Varnhagen acquired learning spanning many languages and fields of the humanities. She read, spoke, or studied German, Greek, Latin, Hebrew, Yiddish, English, Italian, French, Sanskrit, and Turkish (Tewarson, *Rahel* 21). The literature she read exemplifies the western canon: Homer, Dante, Shakespeare, Tasso, Hume, Rousseau, Diderot, and Montaigne; while the contemporary German authors she studied included Goethe, Wieland, Schiller, Tieck, Jean Paul, Friedrich Schlegel, and many others.

When her father died in 1790, Varnhagen took over some domestic responsibilities and authority. Her brother Markus, a year younger than she, was married and lived independently; he took over the business concerns and all financial matters for the family, making Varnhagen and her mother dependent on him for support. Varnhagen took over the education and raising of the younger children.

In the same year as the death of her father, she began to invite a group of people to regular teas; these diverse gatherings to discuss cultural issues primarily in literature and music formed the basis of what is now known as Varnhagen's first salon. Several of her contemporaries in Berlin were also running salons. These were young women of wealthy Jewish families seeking acceptance and cultural exchange with a wide circle of people. The salon followed the style of Moses Mendelssohn, who a generation earlier had worked to liberate Jews "from the spiritual ghetto" and made "his home a meeting place for intellectuals, distinguished foreign visitors, and the Berlin *haute volée*, hoping to promote mutual understanding" (Craig 130). For example, Moses Mendelssohn's daughter, Dorothea Veit (later Schlegel), and also Henriette Lemos Herz (1764–1857) gathered with writers, musicians, and others for evening discussions; however, both Herz and Veit were married and held their salons in the homes of their husbands. Herz, from a similar Berlin Jewish family, entertained in her drawing room with her husband, Markus, a liberally-minded physician interested in arts and letters. In general, the salons that met in this era, unlike the reading circles and learned societies of the earlier half of the century, were run by women. Visitors to the Herz salon admired their hostess for her intelligence, her famed beauty, the well-appointed rooms, and the prestige of associating with her and her husband.

In comparison, Varnhagen might seem to have had less to offer. At the time she first organized a salon on a regular basis, she was nineteen years old, unmarried, and a member of a family that was tolerated for its importance in business more than it was truly respected. Yet her salon competed with the others; she drew regular visitors on the strength and reputation of her superb intellect and tactful social skills. She distinguished her salon by running it on principles of complete egalitarianism, fostering an atmosphere of tolerance and treating poor students with the same respect she showed the princes who frequented the salon. The selection of topics for conversation was not dictated by the hostess, and she phrased her own insights appropriately, humorously, and yet never at a guest's expense. The luminaries who attended her salon included two princes, Radziwill and Louis Ferdinand — who often brought his mistress, the actress Pauline Wiesel — the political analyst Friedrich von Gentz, the Swedish ambassador Karl Gustav von Brinckmann, with whom Varnhagen corresponded for years and whose letters play an important part the in first published collection of her letters, and a host of writers like Tieck, Chamisso, Brentano, and Friedrich Schlegel. This group of well-known personalities frequented the meetings they would have referred to as teas presided over by Mademoiselle Levin and held in an attic room of an apartment she shared with her mother.

Varnhagen herself called the conversations at these aesthetic teas "truths from the garret" (*Dachstubenwahrheiten*).

During the fifteen years in which she conducted the salon meetings, Varnhagen also read, interpreted, and discussed Goethe's literary publications. In 1795, at age twenty-four, she met Goethe while staying at the baths in Teplitz, Bohemia (now the Czech Republic). The Teplitz baths were frequented by many prominent people from across the German regions. This personal meeting with Goethe was brief as were subsequent ones; nevertheless, his importance to her grew steadily throughout her life, and she never tired of proselytizing and advancing his excellence. The appreciation of Goethe's fiction was an especially strong theme in the friendship with Alexander von der Marwitz (1787–1814), limited to five years due to his early death. Varnhagen valued Goethe's ability to express contemporary ideas in his fiction in a way she found to be true, accurate, and in full agreement with her own. She was confident of the longevity and quotability of his works, particularly of Goethe's *Torquato Tasso* and the Wilhelm Meister novels.

After the 1795 holiday in Teplitz and first encounter with Goethe, she returned refreshed to her native city of Berlin. While attending a performance at the opera house, she was introduced to a handsome, young German nobleman and began what was to become a long and painful romantic relationship with the Count Karl Finck von Finckenstein. They were at one point engaged, despite anti-Semitic objections from his family; the engagement with Finckenstein clearly represented a step upward in the social hierarchy as he belonged to one of the leading aristocratic German families. They seem to have been incompatible, and biographers have been compelled to dwell on the contrasts between Varnhagen and Finckenstein; he was blond, handsome, aristocratic, in social settings a wallflower, of mediocre intelligence, and wavering in his views; she was dark (in comparison), of ordinary appearance, insightful, Jewish, a prominent and gracious personality in Berlin social circles, and intensely passionate about her convictions. Varnhagen, torn apart by her love for him and by his inertia, broke off the relationship irrevocably in the spring of 1800.

In the time following the relationship with Finckenstein, Varnhagen traveled from Paris to the Hague. Although she did live for a time in Prague and Vienna, like Arnim, she repeatedly returned to her home, Berlin, the city where she had genuine feelings of allegiance. She lived with her mother for many years, as her other siblings had married and moved out. In 1802, now in her thirties, she met the Spanish diplomat Don Raphael d'Urquijo and experienced her second unhappy love relationship. This one lasted until the summer of 1804 yet in many ways repeated the pain and disappointments of her first love for Finckenstein. D'Urquijo was also

Christian and, although Spanish, had a social position in Berlin and the German countries that an unmarried Jewish woman could not otherwise attain. Although Varnhagen's letters to him have been destroyed, judging by statements made by her and by her husband, who did read the letters, this relationship had a pathological effect on her. Both d'Urquijo and Varnhagen seemed passionate and obsessed. She purportedly broke off all social contact in order to please him and moved to the countryside. He, in a style that sounds as melodramatic as contemporary opera plots, made "jealousy an article of faith" (Tewarson, *Rahel* 65). It is curious to note, however, that she did not decide to convert from Judaism for him and that she broke off the relationship.

In 1806 Napoleon entered Berlin, and, under French occupation, the Levins' fortunes plummeted. The presence of Napoleon and the tumble of the German governing structures disrupted and dispersed Berlin society, bringing a definitive end to the first salon. Varnhagen's nature, however, was to be sociable, and she redirected energy that had gone to the salon toward letter writing and several new and deep friendships. She formed intimate friendships with two women; one with Rebecca Friedländer was cultivated for four years, while the friendship with Pauline Wiesel continued throughout both women's lives much like the enduring friendship between Caroline Schlegel-Schelling and Luise Gotter. "Rahel: a Book of Remembrance," the focus of the following critical interpretation, contains comparatively little thematic material about her friendships with women, while the letters she exchanged with Friedländer and Wiesel provide ample testimony of their importance to her (Tewarson, *Rahel* 81–88). The extant letters have recently been published in separate volumes (Varnhagen, *Briefe an eine Freundin*, and Varnhagen, *Briefwechsel mit Pauline Wiesel*).

In her thirties, at an age when Bettina von Arnim and Caroline Schlegel-Schelling were both mothers and wives, Rahel Varnhagen shared a home with her mother and was supported by her brothers. However, she did take steps that signal her independence: she moved into her own apartment and adopted a different last name, Robert. Her younger brother, Liepman, had already established himself as an author under the name Robert (*RV* 10: 323, 328). Also, at age thirty-seven, she met a student of twenty-three years, Karl August Varnhagen von Ense (1785–1858), who later became her husband; at the time of their initial acquaintance, he was writing fiction, pursuing a diplomatic career, and had another romantic involvement. Meanwhile, she was turning other acquaintances into dear friends, such as Karoline von Fouqué, Heinrich von Kleist, and Clemens Brentano. She also lost friends and family as she approached her fortieth birthday. In 1809 her mother died, while in 1811 Finckenstein died and Kleist committed suicide.

An additional and significant indicator of the move toward autonomy came in the form of her first publication. The publication was also a harbinger of the coming relationship with Karl August, for his name appeared on the work as editor while she remained anonymous. The publication is entitled "On Goethe: Fragments taken from Letters," and it appeared in 1812 in several issues of the *Morgenblatt für gebildete Stände*, a widely read Berlin magazine. Moreover, Karl August had written to Goethe, ostensibly for his permission to publish the excerpts yet simultaneously leaving a clear paper trail to Rahel Levin. A year later, in 1813, after Prussia declared war on France, she and her family departed from Berlin to move to Prague, where sentiment was decidedly against the French. Varnhagen and her Levin relatives returned to Berlin after the defeat of Napoleon, but not until after she had distinguished herself once again. Like Arnim, who actively engaged in socially responsible activities, Varnhagen cared for wounded soldiers in an emergency war hospital in Prague and helped to raise money to support such hospitals. It took a toll on her, however, and she returned to the Teplitz spa to recover her health.

There, she and Karl August decided to marry and to return to Berlin. In anticipation, she converted to the Protestant faith, now using the names Friederike Antonie. The pastor was the humanist reformer and well-known theologian, author of a theory of salon sociability, Friedrich Schleiermacher. On September 27, 1814, she and Karl August wed. Because he was pursuing a career as a Prussian diplomat, they first moved to Vienna for the Vienna Congress of 1815 and then on to Karlsruhe in their second year of marriage. Without an acceptable explanation, Karl August was released from diplomatic service to Hardenberg in 1819. Historians offer the explanation that the liberal political viewpoints which both Varnhagens supported diverged too far from the growing conservatism of the post-Napoleonic era of German government. So, the Varnhagens returned to Berlin, where they revived the social tradition of running a salon she had established earlier. Their relationship was free of the pain that she had experienced earlier with Finckenstein and d'Urquijo, based instead on mutual respect and devoted companionship.

Because of the publications in the Berlin magazine, the Varnhagens' collaboration predates their marriage. In the nineteen years of their marriage, Rahel Varnhagen produced at least ten publications, all of which were officially anonymous, yet she often revealed her authorship to correspondents. Many have titles reflecting their origins in her memoirs and personal letters. In 1816 she wrote "Fragments from Letters and Memorabilia." In 1821, there were two more publications; one was printed in *Der Gesellschafter* on Goethe's novel *Wilhelm Meisters Lehrjahre*, and its author revealed herself only as "Friederike." The second was a more general prose piece in the journal *Die Waage*. In 1826 her "From the Papers of a Contemporary Woman" appeared, also anonymously, while in 1829 she released other excerpts, titled "From the Memoirs of a Berlin woman." Thus, we have evidence that she herself created a public yet unnamed voice from initially private writings.

The second salon also falls under the rubric of her married life, for it was co-hosted by her husband. Officially retired from politics, Karl August increased his cultural standing by becoming a collector, chronicler, biographer, and archivist for important literary figures of German Romanticism. The second salon was attended by Heinrich Heine, Georg Wilhelm Friedrich Hegel, Eduard Gans (a student of Hegel's and an influential legal theorist), the historian, Leopold Ranke, the naturalist Alexander von Humboldt, and numerous international guests, literary writers, musicians, and artists. Varnhagen also corresponded with her noteworthy salon guests, among them, the Jewish poet Heinrich Heine. Unfortunately a fire in 1833 in the apartment of Heine's mother destroyed many of the letters. One letter does appear in *Rahel*, while the collected works contain six additional letters from Varnhagen to Heine (*RV* 3: 443–46 and see 10: 378). In the later years, she welcomed Bettina von Arnim as her guest. There was quite a contrast between their personalities and backgrounds; Arnim was a Catholic, held her husband's aristocratic title as Freifrau von Arnim, was fourteen years younger and a mother to seven children, and loved to act irreverently when in the society of others — yet the two women sustained a friendship. The sole letter from Varnhagen to Arnim that appears in "Rahel: A Book of Remembrance" reflects the mutual respect of shared uniqueness and also a tension resulting from differences (*RV* 3: 512). Arnim's name is suppressed from the publication. In the 1830s, Arnim was also receiving intellectuals for lively conversation in her own salon in her Berlin rooms. The two salons were rather different: Arnim seemed to enjoy turning her meetings into autobiographical monologues. Her friends met irregularly and probably infrequently. The two women, perhaps because of their dramatic differences, recognized the predominant similarity they shared as exceptional, intellectual women.

In many aspects, the second salon resembled Varnhagen's first; for example, the topics of conversation covered a diverse range of cultural subjects; the day and time were set and the frequency of meetings regular; and the guests represented a range of social ranks. However, while both salons would have debated various musical and literary topics, the second included politics, especially comparisons between the Germans and the French. The second salon endured from the Varnhagens' return to Berlin in 1819 until Rahel's death in 1833, just a few years shorter than the first. In 1821, she published some more pieces, which were again excerpts and revisions of her letters primarily about Goethe's fiction. She continued to write fascinating intellectual letters until her death; in these later letters, for example, she debated with her correspondents — and perhaps equally with herself — the merits of political changes, the contemporary situation of Jews, the appeal of Roman Catholicism and Saint-Simonism, the worsening conditions of the working classes in the Polish and German regions, and moral self-improvement.

In this period, many of the important figures of German Romanticism died: Beethoven died in 1827, Hegel in 1831, Goethe in 1832, and Schleiermacher in 1834. Rahel Levin Varnhagen died on March 7, 1833, of a long-term illness. Karl August survived her twenty-five years, until October 10, 1858. The letters she worked with him to edit and arrange in the last years of her life are only a piece of her entire, voluminous oeuvre; however, the work they comprise narrates the story of a self, as the following analysis shows.

Manuscripts and Editions

The text I have used for this study is the reproduction of the 1834 edition by Varnhagen's husband, Karl August, found in the 1983 collected edition of Feilchenfeldt, Schweikert, and Steiner. In the year of his wife's death, Karl August Varnhagen had circulated a manuscript edition of a smaller collection of letters. *Rahel: Buch des Andenkens*, in spite of its great length, is but a selection taken from the larger body of her manuscript letters. Karl August Varnhagen conceived of but never produced a third, expanded edition, which would have included many passages omitted from the first and second versions (Feilchenfeldt and Steiner, "Rahel Varnhagens Werke" *RV* 10: 83–5). *Rahel*, although it is eighteen hundred pages in length, leaves out hundreds of letters Varnhagen wrote and all the replies from her correspondents. The first edition omits many passages from the published letters, and in the third volume many historical letters are rewritten to appear as diary entries or as aphorisms.

After Karl August Varnhagen's death, his niece, Ludmilla Assing, and others published editions of other blocks of her unpublished correspondence, including her exchanges with her husband, with David Veit, Karoline von Humboldt, as well as diaries she kept. These volumes are all collected in the 1983 edition, along with transcriptions of Karl August Varnhagen's annotations of his copy of the first edition.

The majority of Varnhagen's manuscripts became part of her husband's extensive collection, catalogued in 1911 by Ludwig Stern, and originally housed in the Prussian Staatsbibliothek in Berlin, though many individual manuscript letters are in other libraries or in private hands. All the nineteenth century editions were based on this collection. During the course of the Second World War, the collection was moved from Berlin and was thought to be lost but resurfaced in the Jagiellonian Library in Cracow in 1977 (Hertz, "The Varnhagen Collection" 227). For several years these manuscripts were inaccessible to scholars in the West, and hundreds of manuscript letters and other writings are not included in the 1983 collected edition of Feilchenfeldt, Schweikert, and Steiner because they were not available at the time (RV 10: 8–10). Since the release of the collected works, Deborah Hertz published Varnhagen's previously unpublished correspondence with Rebecca Friedländer in 1988, and Barbara Hahn published the correspondence with Pauline Wiesel in 1997.

Though there is no reason to doubt the general fidelity of Karl August Varnhagen's transcriptions, he made many cuts in the letters he selected, and abstracted passages for the collection of aphorisms at the end of the book. To date, no critical historical edition of the "Book of Remembrance" has been published, based on a comparison of Varnhagen's 1834 edition with the extant manuscript letters in the Varnhagen collection. The value of such an edition would be to permit a more definitive answer to the question of how active a hand Varnhagen's husband took in compiling the "Book of Remembrance." Much of Varnhagen's reputation is based upon that edition. Its validity was not seriously questioned until Hannah Arendt began working with the manuscripts in the 1930s. In her judgment, Karl August Varnhagen selected his wife's letters with the intent of effacing her Jewishness and making her seem more patrician and German than she appears in her original letters. Arendt intended to publish a comprehensive edition of Varnhagen's letters based on the manuscripts, which would correct the portrait left by Karl August Varnhagen's edition, but, due to the tragic disruptions of the Third Reich, she was never able to do so (Hertz, "The Varnhagen Collection" 225). The recent publication of Varnhagen's correspondence with Rebecca Friedlander and Pauline Wiesel helps to correct this omission by giving a more complete account of her relationship to the Berlin Jewish community.

In the past two decades, discoveries from the Varnhagen archive have brought about a need to revise the long-held view that the format of the "Book of Remembrance" was largely the work of Karl August Varnhagen. In fact, it appears many of the decisions concerning the selection and final form of the work were made by Rahel Varnhagen, herself, in instructions she gave to her husband before her death (Isselstein, "'Dies ist die Beute!'" 90). Heidi Tewarson writes that "Among the manuscripts are found lists prepared by Rahel, which clearly indicate the finished form of the book — chronological ordering of letters and diary entries" (8–9). Tewarson believes that Karl August Varnhagen's role as editor was more carrying out his wife's final instructions than substantially altering the work through changes made on his own initiative. This discovery has two important implications for critics: first, that whatever omissions may occur in the selection in *Rahel*, they were omissions Varnhagen herself sanctioned, and, second, that *Rahel* does represent a close approximation to the final form the author wished her letters to take.

In this study, I am concerned with *Rahel* as a literary work. For this reason, though not wishing to deny the significance of these historical, philological questions, I do not intend to dwell on them. While I would certainly agree that critics should continue the study of all Varnhagen's surviving work, I disagree that *Rahel* is incomplete, or an inadequate expression of Varnhagen's literary aspirations. Although, as editor, Karl August Varnhagen abridged the work, I do not believe there are any major flaws in his selection. There is good reason to believe that Varnhagen gave her husband directions, which he followed in editing *Rahel*. Furthermore, I believe that the intellectual and aphoristic formulations of *Rahel: Ein Buch des Andenkens* are at the heart of Varnhagen's literary vision.

Varnhagen and the Egocentric Self

The three prodigious volumes of "Rahel: A Book of Remembrance for her Friends" enclose the developmental phases of epistolary self-expression from private manuscript to published correspondence. As the subtitle suggests, the book consists of literary work made out of a women's lifetime of writing. Although well-known to German scholars, this work is imposingly long for the casual reader (1, 800 pages printed in German fraktur script). The book *Rahel* has frequently been read as a first-hand account of life in the Age of Goethe from a female Jewish perspective — indeed an intriguing viewpoint for historians — and it has been seen as a work brought about by the editing work of her husband. Rahel Varnhagen née Levin, hosted two of Berlin's most brilliant literary salons, one in the 1790s and another in the 1820s. Yet more importantly it contains a valuable example of a woman's work expressing and writing her self.

Throughout her letters, Varnhagen is preoccupied or even obsessed with her self. At one point, she states: "Certainly, I am an egoist! I am an ego that has become an I!" She illustrates a key focus in this study: bringing the literary riches of cultural material to the fore through a better definition of the literary correspondence, a form that simultaneously constrains and enables self-expression. Varnhagen's correspondence is a work of art that freezes, explores, and transcends an important moment in communication: it is the moment in which the self extends outward, in the direction of an other, without ceasing to focus on itself. This is the egocentric self. Far less private than the recalcitrant correspondence of Schlegel-Schelling, Varnhagen's correspondence yields a new understanding of autobiographical self-presentation and displays a development of her female self in a realm in which egocentricity becomes a virtue. Varnhagen's self moves out of the emergent historical realm and seeks entrance into a discourse that is capable of pondering truth as eternal and universal. This work of correspondence asks its readers to think abstractly and to see beyond the author to universal aspects of epistemology and then to reapply those philosophical abstractions to the concrete and perhaps bathetic examples of everyday experience. Varnhagen's book is important because it is a striking example of a literary work in which a woman intentionally uses the correspondence genre as a means of self-conscious, public, uncompromisingly literary self-expression.

Despite reliable, scholarly, and even recent evaluations, a comprehensive overview of Varnhagen's writings is still lacking. I feel that the reception history of Varnhagen's work has been more than a little akin to that great masterwork of American Romanticism, the poetry of Emily Dickinson: it is a work, so unfamiliar in its form and presenting so many challenges to the reader, that its full importance long escaped all but a handful of careful readers. As with Dickinson, Varnhagen's work is deceptively simple. It is read as a woman's occasional writing. Dickinson's first readers preferred the prettiest, least challenging of her verses; they mistook the singularity of her literary vision for peculiarity, without being able to fathom her great and often disturbing depths. Similarly, Varnhagen is read for her autobiographical account of her life as a Jewish salon hostess who contributed to the general appreciation of Goethe's works. The vast majority of readers have not yet learned how to read Varnhagen. So, when readers encounter the difficult philosophic soliloquies, they rush through these disturbing digressions, failing to comprehend that they are the heart of the book. In its essence, *Rahel: Ein Buch des Andenkens* is Varnhagen's spiritual autobiography. It is a testament to her struggles with adversity, her heroic pessimism, and enormous aspiration to transcend the adversity of the self and to arrive at a sublime level of contemplation.

After shifting the focus from seeing Varnhagen's writing as occasional letter writing of historical import to profound egocentric speculation, we can understand why Varnhagen writes with more self-consciousness than either Schlegel-Schelling or Arnim.

> If it's true that I am old, then I have carried my youth along with me: nothing alters me more than a dream from thence. With an awakening heart I seized hold there; where should the dream come from? Yes, a single severity of my father, each murder of a youthful moment, still wounds me, deeper and more insightfully, and more full of despair than before. What is

our life, if in its course, the importance and reality of each moment of existence is lost, because it lies in the past?
                    (To Caroline Humboldt, 7 Dec. 1813; *RV* 2: 154)

This is hardly the polite conversation of the salon hostess. It is a metaphysical complaint — a Schillerian meditation on the brevity of youth, a problem that the writer resolves by proposing that we carry our youths with us, that the painful but powerful recollection of the past may be more immediate, more real than the present. The passage rises from pessimism to hope and then returns to gloom with the final, melancholy question, "What is our life, if in its course, the importance and reality of each moment of existence is lost . . . ?" This passage is characteristic of what is central and best in Varnhagen's letters. At her moments of greatest strength, Varnhagen struggles between an intuition of the sublime powers of the imagination and an overwhelming despair at human inability to overcome affliction and adversity. The self-absorbing battle between these two forces is the drama that lies at the center of Varnhagen's autobiography, which she inscribes through a lifetime of letter writing.

Not all of Varnhagen's letters are as intense or reflective as this passage. Before she achieves sublime egocentricity, she frequently passes through mundane self-centeredness. High-strung sensitivity, excessive hypochondria, and a maudlin fascination with the infirmities of aging resound in the three volumes of *Rahel: Ein Buch des Andenkens.* Even in her youngest letters she can be sage and bitter, risk senile superficiality to make brilliant generalizations, and be cantankerous in spirit while healthy in body. The first and second volumes — despite her insistence on innocence and love of simple truth — tell the story of painful experiences, of trials and tribulations, of initiating and sustaining friendships, and above all of survival despite adversity. They offer meditations on her experience one installment at a time. Unique to the personal writing of a woman of letters, however, each installment here is the irregular measure of the personal letter. Each letter is irregular in length of narration and frequency of transmission. The text is unified by her proclivity for bitingly critical, aphoristic writing, which reaches a climax in the third volume of the chronologically-ordered correspondence. Although not all critics would consider the correspondence autobiography proper (Misch, Morris, Olney, and Stanton), the quotation above on the importance of past existential moments asks its readers to interpret the irregular collection of Varnhagen's letters as her lifework, as her unique autobiography.

Readers of her personal letters find a woman writer who is every bit as unusual as she proclaims herself to be. Perhaps, then, dreams and past reality function differently than Varnhagen believes. Perhaps, moreover, it is in the very nature of a dream to keep past moments alive, to recall their pain, and even to heighten the pain. If so, then Varnhagen misunderstands the function of dreams as lessening "the importance and reality of each moment of existence," which works to her own advantage rhetorically. As a misreading, nevertheless, it calls her interpretation of reality into question as well (Hahn, "*Im Schlaf*" 10–17). Most of the interpretations of Varnhagen's dreams rely on the intensifying function of the dream and not on Varnhagen's suggestion that dreams beautify.

> The *I* of Rahel's writing is conceived of as a kind of communication built on reciprocity — and that means truth — which is the sole guarantor of an experience of totality: the concept of the voucher recurs repeatedly in the letters and always in reference to the self-reflective *I*.
> (Bürger, "Arbeit am Ich" 118)

Fortunately, Varnhagen's interest in the nature of reality and the human capability to perceive it truthfully has not escaped her best readers. Her proclivity for self-reflection pinpoints a moment of conflict that is intriguing to critical and casual readers alike and transcends categories of gender and religion.

There are obstacles in the way of producing conversational letters that are also memorable and literary. We have listened to her remarks on youth and maturity. As for her heritage, or what she once termed the "mistake of her birth" — being Jewish, there are two key passages that help the reader to understand her perception of and relationship to Judaism. These passages sketch wide swings of a pendulum, which is typical of her attitude on many other subjects. She problematizes both internal acceptance and external recognition of her Jewishness. The first was written to David Veit in 1795: "I have a fantasy; it's as if a being had stabbed me in the heart with these words in the moment in which I was pushed into this world: 'Yes, you have sensitivity, you see the world as only few others can, so be great and be noble, nor can I take from you your eternal thinking, but one thing was forgotten; be a Jew!'" (*RV* 1: 133). Varnhagen knew, at the very least, how to write the Hebrew alphabet; she recorded a debt her brother owed her using Hebrew characters to spell German words (Kahn 129). Nevertheless, most of her associations with being Jewish are feelings of embarrassment and misfortune (Weissberg, "Writing" 157–73; *RV* 1: 67). The second important utterance on the subject was recorded by Karl August Varnhagen and appears in his prefatory essay to her correspondence: "The one thing that has, for my entire life, been my greatest burden, my bitterest sorrow and misfortune, to have been born a Jew, now I would not miss out on it for any price" (*RV* 1: 43). Again, readers of *Rahel* will find parallels between the writer's ambivalence toward her Jewishness and her femaleness, as they will find the recurrent quest in the letters for a balance between the specificity of private communication and validity of general truths.

An accurate reading of the book must go beyond the acknowledgment of societal ambiguity toward the artistry of women's writing to reach an interpretation of a unique self generated by the letters within that work. In Varnhagen's letters, communication is one defining function of the epistolary self. Although a communicative voice predominates in the first two volumes, it is not the only voice that Varnhagen uses and it is not the sole function of her epistolary activity. As a letter writer, she addresses the conflicts that arise when writing must serve multiple functions. For example, her letters simultaneously communicate information to an addressee and give her an environment in which she develops a written version of the self. In a sense, communication impinges on the process of constructing the same self, especially when communication is the result of conveying discrete pieces of information while the construction of the self is an ongoing epistolary process. Through the repetition and elaboration of the narratives of her letter writing, Varnhagen seeks to elevate the narrating self above the burdens of communicating experience and of describing existence and to produce in its place an epistolary self free to speculate on totality.

It is not surprising that so many of the letters in the book *Rahel* are not addressed to the illustrious attendees of Varnhagen's well-known salons but rather to less famous, more intimate friends. The salonière had a twofold role: to please interpersonally and personally. Scurla reports that Varnhagen was exceptional in the salon:

> As a young woman lacking worldliness and physical attractiveness, who had to forego the political atmosphere of France and France's capital, Rahel was concerned with the progressive development of humanity, and so she and her salon circle strove for improvement in education, character, and humanity in their challenging conversations. Distinction [in Rahel's first salon] was gained only through intelligence and thought. (Scurla 79)

Commenting on her skills in the salon, Clemens Brentano, Heinrich Heine, and Karl Gutzkow tell that Varnhagen's lack of formal education, her lack of worldly experience, and her Jewishness, made her excellence as salon hostess all the more remarkable.

Initially, the correspondence offers an understanding of friendship locked in the letter's power. The theme of friendship occupies Varnhagen off and on through all the three volumes, the forty years that the work's narrative encompasses. In 1794, she expresses her understanding of friendship:

> Don't you see, I really do understand that sort of thing, and when I really strike a chord of truth, then it's as if I'm paying myself a compliment; yet I

only do that, when it's really important for me to know that I've reassured someone, which is practically not possible in this world even though it is a genuine pleasure to do so. *Par parenthèse*, it occurs to me, that this is true friendship; something, you know, that we're always trying to define.

(To Brinckmann, 15 July 1794; *RV* 1: 75)

Despite such recurrent themes, reaching an understanding of the work's overarching concerns is hindered by polarities. Isolating individual passages produces contradictions: is it friendship or egoism? Thus, the critical effort to survey the correspondence as a whole and to reach an understanding of the work's central themes can seem at times impossible. Reading the entirety of the work, however, shows the author vacillating between aggressive egotism and ruthless self-belittlement in order to develop and to display a map of the development of a female self.

As author of the correspondence, Rahel Varnhagen presents a paraphrase of the question the correspondent Varnhagen asks: How can letters preserve the importance and the reality of bygone moments of existence? In response to its own internally constructed concerns, the correspondence transcends its historical origins.

Writing a Public Voice

Given this understanding of the book's genesis, we can read it as the monumental record of Rahel Varnhagen's powers of self-expression that it is. It is not surprising that she worked towards a public reception of her epistolary monument, because her writing employs literary characteristics that few of her contemporaries used. It is written in an uncommon literary form, since it is more of an extended soliloquy of private, often philosophic, speculation, rather than an account of external events in her life that one would expect from a conventional autobiography. Social letters are usually part of a dialog, but Varnhagen's are more properly described as a monolog. The literary monolog, with the addition of diary and aphorism, creates a different dramatic structure from the usual third-person narrative of autobiography, and allows for an unprecedented drama of self-discovery.

As we have seen, though Karl August Varnhagen followed his wife's instructions in producing the finished edition, it is impossible to know exactly how much *Rahel* represents Rahel Varnhagen's ideal selection of her letters. Many letters, such as those she wrote to her brother, Ludwig Robert, were not included. The unpublished letters reveal aspects of Varnhagen's personality not evident in *Rahel*. Feilchenfeldt argues that a complete understanding of Varnhagen should derive from all her surviving writings.

> In her letters to her brother, to the extent that [Karl August] Varnhagen published them and that Ludwig Geiger tried to fill in the gaps in such publications, there can be found a practical side and a pragmatic interest in Rahel's world view, which contrasts surprisingly with the heavily emotional and aphoristically formulated intellectualism of the atmosphere created by her other epistolary images. (*RV* 10: 110–11)

Reading the Varnhagen correspondence in the edition of 1983 gives us a unique opportunity to trace the developmental stages of the correspondence and thereby to mark its transformation from letters to published correspondence. It also makes it clear that whatever the exact form the correspondence might have taken, publication was the Varnhagen's ultimate aim. She wrote letters throughout her life and saved them. She was in the habit, as were many in the period, of rescinding her letters. It was generally held that personal letters belong to or are the property of the letter writer. She kept, for example, her letters to Finckenstein and d'Urquijo and gave them as a bundle to a very select group of readers.

There is much evidence that Varnhagen always thought of the ultimate aim of her letter writing as publication. She cleverly reversed the popular notion of letters as a variety of autobiography: "My life shall become letters" (to Sara von Grotthuß, Dec. 1824; *RV* 10: 38). During an early period in her letter writing, Varnhagen conceived of such a book and commissioned it from more than one letter recipient:

> And when I die, get all my letters — trick them if you have to — from all my friends and acquaintances (and tell K'n, since I'm dead and done in, I command him — not just him — to give them up) — and then straighten them out with Brinckmann. It'll make an original story, and poetic.
> (To von Boye, July 1800; *RV* 1: 208)

> But I want to sort through my letters myself, and do the throwing out; and not in forty or fifty years as you wrote our good friend [Regina Frohberg], rather a lot sooner; I want to be alive, when it gets read.
> (To Karl August Varnhagen, 22 Feb. 1810; *RV* 1: 467)

The letters present Varnhagen as toying with the idea of publishing a correspondence as early as 1800. The second quotation above, from 1810, indicates a change in the conception for the book — a change that was never executed. She never saw the letters in print and the literary executor, unforeseen by the Varnhagen of 1800 and 1810, was neither Brinckmann nor Boye, but Karl August Varnhagen. Varnhagen often presents herself in the book as a reader, as the sort of reader she herself would most like to have:

> ... and you'll always find enough readers among the Germans if only you get in print. The world will always continue to produce such people. I know, what a joy, what a comfort I get from any spark of truth I find in a

piece of writing. Only thus does the past gain a life, does the present gain a stronghold; and an artistic viewpoint from which to be observed.

(To Karl August Varnhagen, 22 Feb. 1810; *RV* 1: 466)

The passage expresses an optimistic faith in the ability of Germany's readers to find whatever spark of truth a piece of literature contains, "if only you get in print." At the time of this passage, Varnhagen was encouraging the literary ambitions of her then suitor, Karl August Varnhagen, although the passage ultimately has more application to herself and ironically reverses her role from reader to writer.

Varnhagen began and participated in the sifting of individual works out of her epistolary oeuvre. Isselstein has observed, "Beyond this, if one considers the already described tables of contents as the most important element, then one definitely gets the impression that Rahel was working for years intensively and purposely toward publication far beyond the occasional appearance in journals or newspapers" ("'Dies ist die Beute!'" 90). The rediscovery of the Varnhagen Manuscript Collection in Cracow has already begun to refocus the critical reception of Varnhagen's letters.

During her lifetime, Varnhagen authorized the publication of excerpts from her personal letters; however, she never signed her name in print but used instead either a pen name, "Friederike," a code initial, "G.," or simply left the piece anonymous. In the seventeen years leading up to this letter (that is from 1812 to 1829), Varnhagen appeared in print no less than eleven times, and most of the publications derived from her letter writing. She took pride in these publications, as evidenced by her repeated recommendations to correspondents to read them. Some of the recommendations approach exhortations in which she points out, to those who would otherwise not have known it, that she was the author.

> In the accompanying volume, pages 207 to 222 are by me (under the title "Unnamed.") Taken from my letters and papers; which never expected to see the light of any day except the one in which they were written. Varnhagen rummages through everything and I'm not sensitive: I find others' labors not much better; and often much worse.
>
> (To Brinckmann, 24 Apr. 1824; *RV* 3: 157)

Beyond granting permission to others for her words to appear in print, Varnhagen personally prepared articles for publication in 1826 and 1829. Isselstein reproduces a letter by Varnhagen to her publisher Elsholtz as proof of Varnhagen's direct involvement in and approval of the publication of her work; the letter also captures Varnhagen's deliberate ambiguity regarding the secrecy of her name as author (Isselstein, "Rahels Schriften I" 24–9). This reticence is interesting. It might by interpreted as a fear of ungenteel and adverse publicity like the fear that inspired Schlegel-Schelling never to publish her letters. But the situation with Varnhagen is much more complex. She dreaded a public readership in her lifetime, no doubt because her social position was already tenuous, due to the many prejudices arrayed against her. But Varnhagen, while fearing premature public notice, always aspired to eventual fame. The barriers she encountered in her lifetime against self-publicizing seem in her letters to have pushed her toward more ambitious, if tortured, celebration of her self.

Isselstein points out that Varnhagen refers to "herself as an author in the third person, probably as a safeguard against unauthorized eyes" ("Rahels Schriften I" 24). *Rahel* has a section that parallels the anonymous publications' technique of using the third-person. In the letters, inspecting her self from the third-person point-of-view, she writes: "but this kind of presentation of her self can be taken (and indeed with sufficient reason) for her character; which however has really fled into the middle of the heart in the face of the raw and false presupposition and of the only too unpleasant appearance of her self" (diary entry, 28 Mar. 1814; *RV* 2: 184–85). On the one hand, Varnhagen insists emphatically on anonymity and suppression of potentially revealing proper names and places: "the same person also asks you this; ... to transform the *V* of such a sentence, which stands for a proper name, into a *G*" (Isselstein, "Rahels Schriften I" 24). On the other hand, Varnhagen concedes the impossibility of total anonymity with unmistakable delight; she is delighted because she is proud of her distinctive style. She speaks of herself in the third person: " ... and thirdly, he has a style much the same as some people have a handwriting that cannot be mistaken. And I had to give to him about all this" (Isselstein 25).

The passage displays two important characteristics of Varnhagen's auctorial anonymity. First, she chooses the simile comparing style to handwriting in order to indicate the scope of the readership for whom her anonymity is impossible. The circle of Varnhagen and Elsholtz's contemporaries who are familiar with her handwriting was sizeable. Varnhagen has a handwriting that is nearly illegible and hence quite easy to recognize. Immediately following her first anonymous appearance in print, Varnhagen established a hierarchy of readers, cultivating an eventually much larger public. She reports on a conversation with Karoline Humboldt after the 1812 publication of her "Über Goethe: Bruchstücke aus Briefen," which was her first publication and which appeared anonymously. Rahel Varnhagen again speaks with self-conscious pride about her writing: "She said to me: one had confided to her — in Weimar, which could only have been Goethe — that the letters were by me, she had wanted to keep it a secret; I said that it wasn't necessary, for if Goethe knew it, then the whole world could know too" (to K. Varnhagen, 4 Nov. 1813; *RV* 2: 143). Varnhagen implies concentric circles of readers in which each wider circle subsumes the readers of the previous one: herself, Karl August, and very intimate friends, then casual acquaintances, and eventually the nameless public; out of the largest circle, she focuses on Goethe and other kindred spirits of contemplative inclination. This is the first of many indications of Varnhagen's literary aspirations. And, in an important sense, a major part of the drama of *Rahel* is the author's striving to find expression and her struggle to create and publish the work itself, which is in large part an account of its own genesis.

A letter of thanks written to an ordinary reader of much the same standing as Karoline Humboldt — that is, an acquaintance representing a more public readership — exposes Varnhagen's cultivation of a concentricity of readers again. The year is 1829 when she was actively publishing her writing and reviewing her massive unpublished oeuvre with a critical (here editorial) eye. As author, she compares herself to Voltaire: "Although I haven't written in years, certainly Voltaire and his peers did not send off more letters and notes than I did in earlier times" (to Antonie von Horn, 11 Oct. 1829; *RV* 3: 396). Elsewhere, she dubs herself "as unique as the greatest manifestation on this earth" or, with coarse self-irony, "a miraculous creature made from I know not what incomprehensible stuff" (*RV* 3: 399). In her letter of 16 Aug. 1827, to Ludwig Robert, she touts herself as one of Hegel's best students: "Recently I got up the courage, when Hegel was at our house, to tell him that I was reading his book: although I don't lack the conviction that I am one of the students who loves and understands it best: or better understands and loves" (*RV* 3: 283). Varnhagen conceives of her ideal readers as her peers and defines peers as the great contemporary writers.

Varnhagen was obsessed with the idea that her work be judged on par with the work of the great poets and philosophers of the age. It is a dark obsession, because circumstances made it nearly inconceivable. Even if she were working in a less seemingly ephemeral medium than the personal letter or had the freedom to write poetry or philosophy, it is difficult to imagine the nineteenth century receiving the Jewish salon hostess as an author on par with Goethe or Voltaire. Thus, Varnhagen's insistence on her personal greatness is all the more audacious. Her voice emerges from these pages with an unfounded ambition comparable to that of Walt Whitman, the casual laborer from Brooklyn who in 1855 declared himself a Cosmos. But Varnhagen's egocentricity is not only more immersed in the public, social world than Whitman's; it is darker, more frustrated and pessimistic. It is as if she has glimpsed a freedom, which she knows she can celebrate, but never possess.

The second important characteristic of Varnhagen as author is her belief in self-recognition and self-delimitation as prerequisites to becoming an author, to which the letters to Elsholtz and von Horn testify. Varnhagen refers to herself in the letter to Elsholtz using the third-person pronoun. In the course of the letter, however, she switches from the grammatically feminine *Person* to the masculine *Schreiber*; more important than the change in grammatical gender is the elevation represented by the difference in meaning, from "individual" to "writer." Varnhagen begins the letter with an oblique self-reference, then expounds a list of textual emendations, and concludes with another oblique self-reference yet one that accords her the status of writer. The letter to Elsholtz thus records the literal transformations a private manuscript must undergo to become a public text. It exposes, simultaneously, the conversion a letter writer experiences in becoming an author.

Unlike other authors whom she envied, Varnhagen did not have much opportunity to respond to letters from appreciative readers. Hence, the letter to von Horn — an instance of this under-represented group — merits close attention. After telling von Horn that Voltaire and his peers could not have written more letters and notes than she, Varnhagen goes on to describe her gradual recognition of her ability as an author. She begins with the initial state of innocence:

> But at that time I didn't know what I was doing: and if I'd thought about it, then it would have been with the following understanding: everyone writes like this and writes as much as occurs to them. I remained in such a state of heaven sent innocence until the very last days of my youth; although at the very beginning, in my twelfth and thirteenth years, my personal notes and family letters generated plenty of discussion and laughter: I firmly believed — such luck! — that it was other people's problem: they were so peculiar; and they could not understand what I wanted to say . . . .
> (*RV* 3: 396)

This conviction of possessing insight that will always fall on the deaf ears of an uncomprehending public is one of the hallmarks of Varnhagen's writing and gives rise to her sense of isolation and abstraction. She then summarizes the years in which her consciousness was raised as a painful experience:

> Since my youth, there was a feeling of richness in me in keeping with truth; Nature had a sharp and acute effect on my sharp senses; gave me a sensitive heart with the firmness of granite that honestly and eternally animated all my other senses; — my head was well made for deeper thought and insight . . . . So it could not have been otherwise than that I drank from all cups and chalices, the bitter and the sharp . . . .
> (to Antonie von Horn, 11 Oct. 1829; *RV* 3: 396).

Genre: The Epistolary Author as Autobiographer of Egocentricity

Varnhagen's correspondence transcends the boundaries of even unconventional literary genres — letter, diary, and aphorism; it sublimates the already tenuous distinctions between narrative modes — autobiography, story, and memoir — and produces in its place egocentric correspondence. The most obvious definition of autobiography subordinates it to the broader heading of biography, holding that the biographer and the author be the same person. Autobiography presumes empathy felt by the reader for the author, which the last part of the subtitle literally stipulates: "for her friends." Another definition of autobiography proposes that it explains "the relation of an individual life to the shared beliefs of its stipulated audience, selecting events from the writer's own past life and arranging them retrospectively into a narrative pattern that simultaneously illustrates the writer's opinions and shows how he came to hold them" (Spengemann 73). This definition proves useful for its first stipulation, that of a covenant between the individual life and the shared beliefs of an invited audience. In Varnhagen's view, those shared beliefs are a covenant of pain: "If one considers another person to be a friend, then he gains no more from this than to be treated as poorly, impolitely, and harshly as one treats one's self . . . " (to Veit, 21 Mar. 1795; *RV* 1: 130).

Varnhagen's goal is to center the focus on her self; to do this, she must work against both the inherent dialogue form of the personal correspondence and against the typical epistolary theme of intimate friendship. Yet she shies away from neither. Instead, she subverts or silences her partners' response and converts the theme of friendship into speculation on her self. It is therefore surprising to find, as a counterpoint to the book's strong egocentric perspective, that "Rahel: A Book of Remembrance" inscribes friendship and the changes friendship undergoes from its eighteenth-century conception to nineteenth-century practice. She thematizes it in the ever-echoing refrain throughout the book, which she takes from Goethe's *Hermann und Dorothea* — "Friends, like-minded." Writing to a female friend, she explains her fascination with Goethe's terse but profound definition: "Friendship is not an empty word! Goethe defines it in his elegy: 'Friends, like-minded, enter here!' and this word has ever struck me; and indeed forever. What are friends? Like-minded ones" (to Frau von Grotthuß, Dec. 1824; *RV* 3: 178). Varnhagen's correspondence is autobiographical insofar as autobiography describes the segments of life that radiate from the individual outward toward others. Christa Bürger also sees Varnhagen's letter writing as marking the experience of a change of epoch: it is the "expression of the experience of an epoch: the experience of a bourgeois intelligence undergoing the transition from traditional to modern society" ("Arbeit am Ich" 116). The inscriptions of friendship begin, not surprisingly, with the strong, central narrating self, only to turn toward the peripheral other.

In comparing the actual form of *Rahel: Ein Buch des Andenkens* to other correspondences, a fundamental difference reveals itself: whereas *Goethe's Correspondence with a Child* represent an exchange of letters, "Rahel: A Book of Remembrance" does not. Although the effect does indeed eliminate dialogue, the result is not *per se* monolog. To guarantee monolog, the Varnhagens found it necessary at times to reform letters into diary entries. Beyond the emergence of a prose self, the result of the Varnhagens' correspondence, then, is an isolation of the way in which one speaker may use dialogue as a means of self-elicitation to generate autobiography. The isolation of one out of two correspondents presents a speaker using epistolary dialogue and friendship as a means of acquiring self-knowledge. The formal change from extroverted epistle to introverted diary draws attention to the first moment of writing: moving from the mental self outward toward a prose self. The following passage derives from an historical letter yet was a likely candidate for change from letter to diary. Although the content is equally appropriate for the more meditative diary, its form in the published correspondence maintains the hallmarks of the dialogic letter: "I returned part of Heinrich Kleist's stories to Schl., and wanted then a book from him, and took Spinoza" (*RV* 2: 38). She continues the monolog:

> I'm reading him now. My whole life long I imagined him to be different. I understand him very well. Fichte is much harder. It is strange; it always seems to me that the philosophers are all saying the same thing; the ones who aren't shallow anyway. They all use different terms, which all — to be honest — mean the same thing . . . . Spinoza is my favorite; his thinking is very honest and attains the most profound absolute and gives it expression; and has the lovely character of the thinker; impersonal, gentle, quiet; occupied with and emerging from the depths.
> (To Marwitz, 9 Apr. 1812; *RV* 2: 38–39)

The transformation of what were at one time historical letters to pseudo-diary entries in the published correspondence makes irrelevant the identity of the letter's historical recipient. Instead, her egocentric self generates discourse for its own speculative enjoyment. The transformation strips away any passive conformation Varnhagen's mental self might have undergone in assimilating itself to an apostrophized other and bares in its place an apparently self-focused, discursive self that actively shapes material for its own sake and that generates discourse on ideas for their philosophical worth.

The author, as a consequence of her role as egocentric autobiographer, pivots around her self, producing a tone that swings from aggressive egocentricity to ruthless self-belittlement. The much-quoted passage that begins with a proclamation of her greatness turns to painful resignation:

> I am as unique as the greatest manifestation on this earth. The greatest artist, philosopher or poet is not above me. We are of the same element. On the same level, and belong together. Whoever would exclude others would exclude himself. But life was chosen for me; and so I remained in embryo, up until my century; outwardly, I am entirely submerged, that's why I say it myself. So that an image concludes my existence. Indeed, agony, as I know it, is also a life; and I think that I am one of those creations that humanity ought to toss away, no longer needs and no longer can. No one can console me. (To Veit, 16 Feb. 1805; *RV* 1: 266)

In another passage in diary form, the pendulum reverses from low to high: the egocentric self swings; "just as some people do not have a single pretty trait in their faces, or a body proportion that is not praised, and nevertheless make a favorable impression . . . it is for me the reverse," and "my vanity is above all else; that's what I hold my indignation to be" (diary entry 29 May 1811; *RV* 1: 510–11). She strikes a balance only amongst "friends, the like-minded." In between the extremes of self-annihilation and self-aggrandizement, she repeats her adherence to Goethe's definition of friendship and details her own understanding of it:

> "Friends! Like-minded!" Goethe exclaims in his elegy. An exclamation has never moved me more deeply. He is a definition: and he already existed in my soul. Welfare — *charity*, love — we have and should have for every sort of human being and creature. Friendship, respect, agreement — these we can only have toward the "like-minded." From such, we know that they unwaveringly desire the same principal points as we do, that not for a moment would vanity or the lust for victory disturb, endanger or interrupt these great points. Then everything is right. Intelligence, talent, humor, mood, knowledge, capabilities, attractiveness, these are all additional . . . .
> (To Fräulein von R., 22 Aug. 1827; *RV* 3: 286–87)

As autobiographical correspondence, *Rahel: Ein Buch des Andenkens* thematizes discursively the triangulation inherent in the relational and connective modes of historical epistolarity (Altman; Kauffman; Farrell).

An obsession with letter style and anticipation of readers' likely responses characterizes volume three. If this were not sufficient to establish Varnhagen's self-portrait as an artist, the correspondence reverses the ratio of epistolary texts to diary entries. In addition, aphorisms begin to precipitate from the diaristic segments, although many retain the personal pronoun:

> The fear of God derives from the idea that we all descend from him and all are equal, and ought to be treated equally good and equally bad! Every day I get more and more proof of the fact; that a feeling heart is a

gift from God: that opens the portals of such a view; that's the talent I have possessed. But, this is also my only talent; in the place of all the ones I don't have. O what a surrogate! (Diary entry, Mar. 1829; *RV* 3: 384)

Meditating on her artistic talent leads Varnhagen to an elevated level of self-consciousness. Her sense of her own uniqueness reaches, at times, ridiculous and sentimental heights. Reading a small section of Varnhagen's correspondence (five letters to Marwitz from April to June of 1810), Vigliero examines Varnhagen's acute sense of self and finds the same swings from the sublime to the ridiculous (52–55). In response to a "long, chatty, and divine" letter written to the Varnhagens by the much-idolized Goethe, she sighs: "a horn would grow out of my forehead, except that I'd have cried it away" (to Ludwig Robert, 13 Apr. 1825; *RV* 3: 195). This peculiar remark about herself not only anticipates that readers will find her unique, but also supplies them with a symbolic comparison to the mythological and unique unicorn with an extra measure of pathos. Varnhagen's letter writing continues it development toward more intense self-reflection. For example, soon after the image described above, a passage appears with the oxymoronic heading "Orally" in parenthesis, which is relativized by appearing in parenthesis, and the date stands in diary fashion at the end of the entry. Moreover, unlike most diarists, she represents herself through a third-person reference and presents her own words as quoted speech of another.

> Sunday morning, in the little garden, with the warmest Spring breeze, when the branches were just about to turn green; we had spoken about how life sometimes makes the familiar seem foreign . . . at that moment Rahel called out painfully with melancholy grief: "Alas, we are but a drop of consciousness. And I want so very much to return to the sea — why must I be special!" (*RV* Diary, 24 Apr. 1825; 3: 194–95)

The passage carefully sets the scene for intellectual speculation: in the best peripatetic manner, not unlike philosophical treatises couched in dialogue form, the interlocutors tour a garden in the spring, standing at the threshold of burgeoning nature and their own developing consciousnesses. An initial interpretation might name the interlocutors Rahel and Karl August. While this is not inaccurate, we can better interpret the overarching enterprise of the book and make sense of its apparent contradictions by comparing that passage to the very next entry:

> "Certainly I am an egoist! I am an *ego* that has become an I!"
> What an atrocious confession! And you are proud of it?
> "That depends on interpretation: it depends, that is, on what we understand. The more you restrict your *I*, the more obvious your limitations are, the more agility you allow it in vulgar pleasures, all the more intolerable it will become to other *I*'s and all the more of a burden (in the most profound sense of the word) to itself: but, to concede more to all the other

I's than to one's own is a distortion or a lie, certainly against our self. Now do you understand my atrocity somewhat better?" (Diary entry of 28 Apr. 1825; *RV* 3: 195; Varnhagen's quotation marks)

Formal indecision marks the first entry, while its tone is one of philosophical certainty. The text of the second entry does not reproduce the descriptive scenery of the first; however, the punctuation and pronouns suggest that the reader is to apply the same symbolic setting to its similarly imagined dialog. Varnhagen's utterances appear in quotation marks: "Certainly I am an egoist! I am an *ego* made into an I!" Since the words of the second speaker, as it were, do not appear in quotation marks and since the title "orally" has been stricken from this entry, the interlocutor is no longer Karl August or some walking partner. Here we have a conversation between Varnhagen and Varnhagen, between the salonière and the letter writer, or between the author and her autobiographer. There is an initial reference to herself in the third person: "then Rahel called out painfully in melancholy grief . . . " (*RV* 3: 195). Although it is in general difficult to distinguish an author Varnhagen from a character Rahel in the first entry, this grammatical reference implies such an interpretation. In the second, furthermore, she shows clearly that she, an author, has split her self into two without alienation. It is convenient for her exploration of her ego to center her writing on that ego by herself. Most appropriately, then, the second entry represents a conversation between Varnhagen's ego or mental self and her *I* or written self.

In *Rahel*, it is Rahel Varnhagen who speaks brilliantly and at length. Some epistolary authors, such as Arnim, view their letters as overcoming an unbridgeable gap between self and other; consequently Arnim emphasizes the connective power of epistolary writing and uses it to cultivate friendship and to keep love alive. Varnhagen, however, does not accept this conception of letter writing. Thinking like an analytic philosopher and writing with the metaphoric language of a poet, she writes to her sister that distance from a friend is death: "I am so saddened, my dear Rose, that you have lost friends to death; and through a half-death, through distance. One can't regain them as quickly" (to Rose, 15 Nov. 1823; *RV* 3: 127). The passage above typifies Varnhagen's pattern of reformulating more tersely ideas that had occurred to her earlier. Compare the concise formulation above that calls separation (literally, "distancing") a "half-death" to the verbose, indulgent, yet equally characteristic articulation of the very same idea in the passage below:

> The waves of life sneak up, race, storm, surge over, and if friends are not sitting together in one and the same ship, not on one and the same bank, then it will be in vain to try to fish them out; even when caught they are dead, single, without current, without meaning, life or relationship. For

that reason separation is so harsh: for the *cleverest* of people as for the others, because then communication stagnates . . . .
 (To Karoline von Schlabrendorff, 22 July 1820; *RV* 3: 28)

Varnhagen returns above to the issue of friendship maintained at a distance — one of the crucial enterprises of letter writing — yet her style shows her groping here for the perfect word, the *mot juste* that elsewhere does not elude her writing. Conscious of her rhetoric, she extends the metaphor of friendship as a boat on the sea of life. What she fears most is not the catastrophic shipwreck; the outcome matters. Because she values togetherness, she imagines the friends in the same lifeboat, washing up on the same bank. Varnhagen refrains from praising the letter as uniting two friends, not because she is unaware of the act of writing, but because her consciousness is so acute that it recognizes that union presupposes separation and distance. Certainly the letter can conjoin, and she is not disturbed that such an epistolary conjunction would be contrived. She fears, more than textual separation and distance, silence. She is afraid that the transference of communication that letters represent may fail her; she trembles when "communication stagnates." And so, the letter writer writes on, and the correspondence is propelled not by plot but by the desperate need to utter in order to survive. The segments of the correspondence, which are primarily letters but sometimes diary entries or aphorisms, are motivated into what could be called the narrative of the text by the discursive and excursive representation of the writer's self. This is her version of egocentricity.

It is therefore neither surprising nor contradictory to read passages on friendship that begin with the strong, central narrating self and only turn toward the peripheral other. Instead of isolating communication between the first and second persons, Varnhagen's epistolary writing freezes, explores and elevates to transcendence the moment in which the egotistical self extends outward. Printing only Varnhagen's letters presents a speaker using epistolary dialogue and friendship as topics, as a means of self-elicitation to generate her egocentricity. With the burden of communication removed, she can speculate abstractly on her ego.

The ultimate form of closure in any life narrative is death. What I am calling Varnhagen's egotism, her obsession with her self, extends to a desire to anticipate and describe not only the creation but the extinction of her self. The autobiographical correspondence has access to narrative strategies otherwise denied to autobiography. The positive attributes — that is the actual matter which it presents — permit us to notice the presence of narrative frames. For example, as Nägele points out, autobiography, in which "the subject, as I, ascertains his or her life history, takes hold of it, and thus constitutes a horizon of meaning for him- or herself," has thus taken on a peculiarly insurmountable task: "The subject who would like to take hold of his or her life history finds at least two insurmountable limits: the beginning and the end of the story are inaccessible to the reflective glance. No subject can reflectively reconstruct his or her birth, even less his or her death" (Nägele 25–26). The author Varnhagen anticipates and prepares readers for her death both in form and content in ways unavailable to most authors. Each letter opens and closes, and each letter animates and silences her; she signs on and off. In that the letter is a sign of her life history, each conclusion stands for her death, and each new salutation signals her birth. In addition, Varnhagen's obsessive hypochondria and thoughts about her own mortality successfully anticipate death and fill in the absence left by the missing and impossible reconstruction of the event on the last page of the book.

The number of diary entries grows in volume two and accelerates in three; they present Varnhagen as reader of other authors, most often of Goethe — yet as interpretive reader. The diary entry identifies its central issue as contradiction and moreover as the individual's disagreement with an overall presentation of the system of understanding. She writes that the individual who disagrees with the systematic but who cannot articulate that disagreement feels a kind of pain, "a lively being that is one living entity with us, a to-us-belonging, as a dead thing, a killed thing" (diary entry Feb. 1833; *RV* 3: 597–98). Combined with the passage immediately preceding this, the conclusion to *Rahel* is nothing if not appropriate, artistic, and literary. The buoyancy of the first text, its dynamic dialogicity, neatly counterbalances the last text's profound contemplation of author and reader, of reader and interpreter, of writing and silence, and of life and death.

The last two texts of *Rahel* recapitulate the central concerns of the entire correspondence. Each text, no more than a paragraph in length, repeats the dichotomies of interpretation sketched out by Varnhagen's book of literary correspondence. In the penultimate entry, a letter, Varnhagen addresses her sister-in-law Ernestine Robert in a personal letter. The first sentence reminds the reader that Varnhagen is weak and dying and simultaneously touches on the abstract idea that the close of a letter symbolizes the letter writer's death, from which recovery is possible: "Your music yesterday brought me back to life: and I am filled with desire for it!" (*RV* 3: 597). The letter has energetic tone, European diction, and extravagant punctuation — "I have tasted blood; I must have more. *Parole d'honneur*! I wanted to invite you even without the Blankensees." The letter also leads to the difficult conclusion to the work.

> ... when a belief has more persuasiveness, when its connections are deeper and richer, when it speaks to and corresponds with our talents, it is all the more difficult to summarize it and to totalize it as a single, coherent ma-

chine: however, every system strives to become such a machine: there exists only one great and living Organized: the created and still self-creating world. (Diary entry Feb. 1833; *RV* 3: 598)

The ultimate entry reveals Varnhagen as reader and author at the same time, as one who reflectively reconstructs her prose self. In Varnhagen's words, "the Organized" exists and is "great and living." Yet it perches on a contradiction: the world is both created and creating. Varnhagen's parting words thereby give rise to a sense of closure that conspires against its own finality. She despairs at her own failure to create a work — which she refers to, somewhat bizarrely as a machine (*Maschine*) — which can summarize and totalize a life's insight. Yet, at the same time, she is reassured that her personal failure does not entirely matter, that the sublime order, the "only one great and living Organized," exists and thrives in a realm beyond human failings and suffering.

4: The Loving Self: Bettina von Arnim

Bettina von Arnim (1785–1859) was the most successful of the three women of letters in this study. Not only did she host a famous literary salon in Berlin and become a confidante to many of the major cultural figures of her age, but she published several volumes of her letters and political writings during her lifetime. Her letters were widely read by her contemporaries and established her as one of Germany's most recognized women writers in the nineteenth century. She made her reputation by refusing to compromise. She earned the censure of many for her unwillingness to live by the strictures of polite society. Her own brother, a recognized poet, once instructed her to suppress publication of her letters on the grounds of propriety. She was a lifelong advocate of freedom of conscience and expression, and progressive causes in education and politics. Although famous in her day for her political activity and her friendship with the poet, Goethe, her most memorable works are her remarkable rhapsodies to the powers of Romantic love contained within the letters she wrote over a lifetime of self-discovery.

Unlike Caroline Schlegel-Schelling and Rahel Varnhagen, both of whom died without children, Bettina von Arnim, one of nineteen children, had seven children of her own. Her father, an Italian by birth, Peter Anton Brentano (1735–1797), was a successful wholesale merchant in Frankfurt and married his second wife, Maximiliane von La Roche (1756–1793), Arnim's mother, in 1774. The discrepancy in the ages of her parents was striking — when they married, Maximiliane was eighteen years old and Peter Anton, thirty-nine. Like his first wife, she was Roman Catholic, but from an established German family, accepted in Frankfurt society. In 1777, Brentano advanced in standing in Frankfurt to become an accredited resident and receive the title, privy councillor. Maximiliane Brentano née von La Roche, mother of Bettina von Arnim, although she did not write herself, had many links to important figures in German literary history. As a young woman, Arnim's mother was admired by Johann Wolfgang von Goethe, before he wrote the novel *Die Leiden des jungen Werthers* (1774; translated as *The Sorrows of Young Werther*, 1779), which was to propel him to international fame. Scholars trace a distinctive feature of that novel's heroine — her beautiful black eyes — to the teenage Maximiliane von La Roche. In addition, Maximiliane was the daughter of Sophie von La Roche (1731–

1807), a major woman novelist in Germany, who held a notable salon and wrote several novels which have recently received considerable attention from feminist critics, including *Geschichte des Fräuleins von Sternheim* (1771; translated as *The Adventures of Miss Sophie Sternheim*, 1776). Maximiliane von La Roche's son, Clemens Brentano (1778–1842), became a widely recognized and anthologized Romantic poet. His works include the poem "Zu Bacharach am Rheine" ("To Bacharach on the Rhine"), known as the Lore Lay poem from the autobiographical novel *Godwi* (1801) and the short story, "Geschichte vom braven Kasperl und schönen Annerl" ("The Story of Brave Kasper and Beautiful Anne," 1817). He also co-wrote with Achim von Arnim a collection of folk verse titled *Des Knaben Wunderhorn* (*The Boy's Magic Horn*) in the years 1805 to 1808. Maximiliane herself stands as the member of the family line who did not write.

In 1785 she had her seventh child, christened Catharina Elisabetha Ludovica Magdalena, and called Bettina. Bettina von Arnim's mother died after the birth of her twelfth child, when Bettina was just eight. Her father, who had outlived two wives, was ensconced in Frankfurt business and local government and spent little time with the young children, although Arnim wrote of him with nostalgic fondness. He remarried a third time after the death of Arnim's mother, to a young woman, Friederike Anna von Rottenhof (1771–1817), and fathered two more children.

In her early years, Arnim reports being singled out as her father's favorite child. Nonetheless, at age eight, she was sent with three sisters to board and be educated in a Catholic school, the Ursuline Convent in Fritzlar near Kassel. Arnim seems to have thrived there; however, much later, when she had adopted Rousseau's naturalist theories of education, she reported critically on her education. It was a conservative, Catholic institution, highly religious and short on rigorous scholarly learning. Arnim retrospectively judged the education at the convent to be dominated by superstition and rote learning (Schultz 5).

When their father passed away unexpectedly in 1797, the Brentano sisters were brought home from the convent. The elder siblings decided that Bettina, Lulu, and Meline (ages twelve, ten, and nine, respectively) would be raised by their grandmother, Sophie von La Roche, the novelist. La Roche lived in a house that she had given the fanciful name *Grillenhütte*, Whimsy Cottage, and had an influence on Arnim's later Bohemian habits. Arnim portrays herself in this period as a tomboy, a girl who cast off the constraints of civilization in favor of uncontrived nature, the nature of her own spirit and the natural world around her. The adult Arnim clearly wanted to let it be known that she led a wild, carefree childhood like Goethe's Mignon, a character from *Wilhelm Meisters Lehrjahre* (1796). Others confirm her penchant for telling tall tales and climbing trees.

Together with the grandmother lived two older women, Sophie von La Roche's widowed sister-in-law and a daughter who was separated from her husband. The Brentano sisters lived there for about five years, from 1797 to 1802. In those years, in her grandmother's household, Arnim came into contact with writers and literary luminaries and was exposed to progressive ideas about women's education and art. She read the Romantic poets and probably learned of the political ideals of the French revolutionary, Mirabeau.

In this period, Arnim's brother Clemens had already established his literary reputation. Arnim and her brother had to become reacquainted, since the seven years between their births resulted in long periods of separation during their upbringing. Clemens had also spent some years at La Roche's with the elderly aunt; however, his residence with his grandmother did not overlap with his sister's. Clemens encouraged Bettina's preciosity, her antics, and the unstructured but intensive development of her artistic character. He took her side, even writing to his friend Ludwig Achim von Arnim that the rest of the Brentano family was mistreating her. Much later in life, Arnim wrote a work of correspondence that derived from the letters she and her favorite brother exchanged, and she published it in 1844 under the title *Clemens Brentano's Frühlingskranz* (Clemens Brentano's Spring Garland).

In 1801 Arnim befriended Karoline von Günderrode (1780–1806). Günderrode was similar to Arnim in that both women had aristocratic ancestry yet the aristocrats had lost their wealth, and both were without parents. Günderrode, however, was five years older and living independently in a home for women in her situation. Arnim was still dependent on her oldest half-brother for support and guidance. Arnim cast Günderrode into the role of intellectual mentor, cherished friend, and poetic inspiration. Günderrode and Arnim's friendship broke off only a few years after it began; in hindsight, Arnim realized that her friend intentionally dissolved the bond. Günderrode was involved — unknown to Arnim — in an unhappy love affair with a married man, Friedrich Creuzer, a professor at Heidelberg, and seemed in hindsight to be anticipating the hurt Arnim would experience when she would have to leave her. Günderrode committed suicide in 1806. Like the special role her brother Clemens played in her development as an artist, this relationship was also meaningful for both her biography and her literary career. Arnim published a work of correspondence based on her relationship and personal letters exchanged with Günderrode, titled simply *Die Günderode* (1840; translated as *Correspondence of Fräulein Günderode and Bettina von Arnim*, 1861); additionally, she included the story of the same-sex friendship in the Goethe book.

In 1802, Arnim moved back to Frankfurt am Main, the seat of the Brentano family. In Frankfurt, she met for the first time Ludwig Achim von Arnim, a student friend of her brother's, and found him quite attractive. It would be nine years, however, until the relationship led to marriage. In the early years of the nineteenth century, Arnim was approaching twenty years old, accustomed to independence of action and thought, yet without a calling in life. Unlike her sisters, she was not getting married and, unlike her brothers, she was not training for a career in business or literature. It was in this period that she became notorious for her intellectual independence and her Bohemian behavior, behavior many acquaintances saw as peculiar and offensive. In the drawing room she poked fun at others' habits and speech. In the spirit of Rousseau, she loved to immerse herself in nature, climb trees, wander along the Rhine and through the fields and forests of the German countryside, spending days and nights out of doors. Some of these wanderings are recounted in the opening letters of *Goethe's Correspondence with a Child*. These encounters with nature and Arnim's fondness for relating them to her friends had drawn her closer to Karoline Günderrode. Günderrode, however, began to distance herself from Arnim; as a consequence, Arnim transferred her affections and her attentions to another poet-mentor. She chose — deliberately after reading the few love letters he wrote to her mother before she had married her father — the great poet, Goethe. He was much admired by her brother Clemens and her mentor Günderrode, the two people whose literary judgments most strongly influenced Arnim at this point. Without meeting him in person, while living in Frankfurt, she cultivated a privileged friendship with Goethe through her personal visits to his mother, from whom she coaxed anecdotes about the poet's childhood, and she eventually parlayed that relationship into a correspondence with the poet.

The relationship she developed with Goethe through her letters was successful enough to elicit his permission to address him as *du*, the familiar "you" form in German (a strong indication of friendship or intimacy), and, in five years' time, an extended personal visit in which he showered attention on her. Arnim achieved these privileges — and indeed they were construed as privileges not only by her but also by Caroline Schlegel-Schelling, Rahel Varnhagen, and many others who knew Goethe — partly because of her befriending Goethe's mother, partly because of her deceased mother, and substantially because of the originality and emotion of her personal letters. In the letters exchanged with Goethe, she took on several roles stretching from the asexual, inspirational muse to a flirtatious young woman dallying with a sentimental middle-aged man, assuming the persona of his androgynous literary character Mignon from *Wilhelm Meisters Lehrjahre*. Arnim's self-stylization reached one peak in her early twenties; she would return to this effort again in her fifties. The work she composed from this correspondence, as we shall see, is a celebration of the grandeur of Romantic love.

In the nearly thirty years that separate the two periods of intentional self-stylization, Bettina Brentano became Frau von Arnim, wife and mother. Arnim married Ludwig Achim von Arnim at the age of twenty-five, and they stayed married until his death. Together, they had seven children. At the same time, Arnim continued to act independent of social decorum and to defy her contemporaries' expectations for polite behavior. Arnim's contrary spirit made itself manifest both in how she went about getting married and in her conduct during her married life. The Arnims eloped on March 11, 1811; the only witness to the ceremony was the elderly wife of the minister who married them, and Arnim returned to her sister and brother-in-law's, where she kept from them the fact of her marriage for five days. Eloping was a means of avoiding traditional wedding festivities — it was not a surprise to her family that she and Ludwig Achim married. Also, they married after she had reached the age of majority and could do so without consent from her guardian. The couple gave their children unusual old Germanic names: Freimund (1812), Siegmund (1813), Friedmund (1815), Kühnemund (1817), Maximiliane (1818; named after Bettina's mother, an exception), Armgard (1821), and Gisela (1827). They spent their honeymoon traveling, as was customary, and visited Goethe.

Arnim had visited Goethe in Weimar twice before her marriage, both times in 1807. Additionally, they had encountered one another in the summer of 1810 while on vacation in Teplitz. Each of these visits accelerated her already growing enthusiasm for Goethe as a confidant and as a writer. When the Arnims married in 1811, they both enjoyed and cultivated Goethe's friendship. Although Goethe unquestionably held center stage from Arnim's perspective, other artists of various sorts had assembled in Weimar in conjunction with Duke Karl August's court and Goethe's entourage and engaged in a stimulating society, with teas, dinners, conversation groups, reading circles, theatrical productions, and museum exhibits. The newlywed Arnims visited Weimar from the end of August to the middle of September in 1811. Unfortunately for Arnim and her much-treasured relationship to the poet, she had a public falling out with Goethe's wife, Christiane, and Goethe unquestioningly took his wife's part. The minor difference of opinions concerned art works on exhibit, yet it had far reaching consequences because Goethe cut off all contact with the Arnims, an ostracization that he maintained without exception for twenty years, despite repeated apologies from Arnim. In the four years before her marriage and before the break, she had sent him forty-one letters, and he had responded — with seventeen — nonetheless very encouragingly. Arnim treasured her former privileged relationship to Goethe and wanted a reconciliation. Goethe's wife died in 1816, and, although he condescended in the 1820s to receive Arnim a few times in his home along with other guests, he remained unreconciled. Between 1817 and 1832, she sent nine letters, none of which he answered. Goethe permitted one of Arnim's children, Siegmund, to call on him in his home in Weimar; the visit turned out to take place just a week before Goethe's death in March of 1832.

Much of the time during the years of her marriage was spent bearing and raising her seven children. Arnim broke with standard practice by encouraging physical activity and social freedom; she taught her children to swim, outfitted them in a peculiarly simple style of homespun clothes, eschewed traditional forms of discipline and punishment, and generally raised them in a manner in fitting with her radical social ideals. While Ludwig Achim struggled to keep the estate operating and profitable in Wiepersdorf, an aristocratic residence of the Arnim family, Bettina and six children moved back and forth between a number of Berlin apartments, which Bettina often rented with the children, while leaving her husband to manage the estate and to have peace to devote himself to his writing.

In this period, she pursued writing, painting, and music, searching in retrospect for an outlet for her artistic creativity. She visited some of the Berlin salons, especially Rahel Varnhagen's. Arnim and Varnhagen became friends on the basis of their shared appreciation for Goethe's works and their mutual respect for each other's hard-fought social and intellectual independence. When she reached age fifty, Arnim's life reached a turning point in several respects. Her husband, Ludwig Achim, died on January 21, 1831. Goethe died in 1832. And a year later she suffered a third bereavement with the death of her friend, Rahel Varnhagen, in many respects a similarly unique woman and independent thinker. Her social and personal life was changed, leaving her more independence than ever and a surviving priestess in Goethe's service — a source of oral history for the bygone movement of German Romanticism. The turning point was also marked by the appearance of her first published book, *Goethe's Correspondence with a Child*, which became a literary sensation. That publication, in turn, marked Arnim as a personality and gained her admirers from a younger generation. Like Varnhagen and Schlegel-Schelling, Arnim conducted a salon, in Berlin from the mid 1830s for approximately a decade. She could name among her friends many major cultural figures, including the musicians, Ludwig van Beethoven, Felix and Fanny Mendelssohn, Robert Schumann, and Johannes Brahms. Often her salon evenings included instrumental and vocal concerts. It was not, however, the intimate group of collaborators that Schlegel-Schelling gathered around her in Jena; nor was it the regular meetings of conversation shared by open minds despite disparities in social hierarchy that Varnhagen presided over in her salon evenings. Arnim at times attended Varnhagen's aesthetic teas. However, she preferred her salon to grow out of her programmatic refusal to accept social conventions and her habit of running an open house with her children, her friends, and her visitors. When the number of unfamiliar visitors increased due to the public's admiration for her Goethe book, her apartment developed into an unofficial forum to appreciate Goethe's greatness, to discuss Romantic concepts of nature, and to listen to Arnim holding forth in charming, poetic, and probably embellished anecdotes about her life and experiences. Ultimately, Arnim's salon grew to concern the subject that was increasingly occupying her attention — politics and social reform.

Especially significant was the affair of the Göttingen Seven, which included her friends, the brothers Grimm, the linguists, anthologists of German folklore, and first authors of the definitive historical dictionary of the German language, who became involved in a controversial protest against the autocratic Hanoverian monarchy in 1837. The decade from 1838 to 1848 was a time of tremendous political ferment as nationalism, democracy, constitutionalism, and revolution were debated and attempted within Prussia and greater Germany. Arnim's oeuvre includes also several works that testify to her political and social engagement; she published two political tracts during her lifetime: *Dies Buch gehört dem König* (This Book is the King's, 1843) and *Gespräche mit Dämonen* (Conversations with Demons, 1852), and a third was published posthumously in 1962 as *Bettina von Arnims Armenbuch* (Bettina von Arnim's Book of the Poor).

From the age of fifty onward, Arnim became an active writer at a level she had previously not attained and with impressive success. She assisted Wilhelm Grimm and Karl August Varnhagen in editing her husband's collected works and the literary papers left by her brother, Clemens Brentano. She and Karl August Varnhagen were well acquainted; as his notebooks attest, he supported her literary projects, and she consulted him regularly to find a sympathetic ear for her political activities. Her final years were much occupied with publishing her literary papers. Her first book established her as a literary sensation; *Goethe's Briefwechsel mit einem Kinde: Seinem Denkmal* first appeared in German in 1835 (translated into English by the author and others and published just two years later as *Goethe's Correspondence with a Child*). In addition, she composed three other epistolary works to make a total of four books that blur the border between fiction and nonfiction. In 1840, the second correspondence, *Die Günderrode*, appeared; then came *Clemens Brentano's Frühlingskranz* (Clemens Brentano's Spring Garland), in 1844, and *Ilius Pamphilius und die Ambrosia* (Ilius Pamphilius and Ambrosia), a letter exchange with a Berlin student, in 1847–48. She was not the only writer engaged in this sort of epistolary creativity; her friends Pückler-Muskau and Karl August Varnhagen were also publishing personal correspondences, based to varying degrees on historical exchanges. Arnim, however, excelled at self-construction and publication.

The number and the success of each of these literary works accorded Arnim an acceptance as a writer that literary history has been reluctant to grant to Schlegel-Schelling and Varnhagen. The diversity of her abilities and her success are manifold; the stone monument to Goethe which she designed and for which she raised money through the sale of her Goethe book was erected in Weimar in 1853, when she was sixty-eight — although she sharply criticized the artistry of the final statue. She continued to make use of her talents, writing fairy tales and composing music in addition to editing her own collected works, as *Sämtliche Schriften* (1853), which reprinted six of her previous publications: the Goethe book, *Günderrode, Königsbuch, Frühlingskranz, Ilius*, and *Dämonen*. All these activities slowed after a debilitating stroke a few years before her death, and, although she recovered partially, she spent the remaining time in Berlin, being cared for by her children. She died on January 20, 1859, leaving an exceptional life behind her, having fashioned herself into a self-made woman of letters.

Manuscripts and Editions

Arnim is the most studied of the three women letter writers. She published most of her works during her lifetime, produced her own collected works, and, in addition to numerous individual reprints, her works have gone through four scholarly collected editions: those of Waldemar Oehlke (1920–22), Heinz Härtl (1986–89), Gustav Konrad and Joachim Müller (1959–63), and Walter Schmitz and Sibylle von Steinsdorff (1986 to the present). The most recent publication of Schmitz and Steinsdorff is an excellent historical-critical edition, which I have used in this study as the basis for my translations. They use as their copy text Arnim's first edition with a small number of textual emendations and modernization of spelling, while attempting to preserve Arnim's distinctive punctuation and other orthographic peculiarities.

The crucial philological question concerning Arnim's *Correspondence with a Child* is to identify which portions of the published work originated in the historical letter exchange and which portion resulted from Arnim's extensive emendations made after Goethe's death. A detailed answer to this question is possible, thanks to the state of surviving manuscripts. Most of the historical letters written between 1807 and 1832 have survived and are reproduced in the Schmitz and Steinsdorff edition so they may be readily compared with the text of the 1835 *Correspondence with a Child*, which contains numerous departures from the original letters. Arnim recovered her original correspondence with Goethe after his death and a collection consisting of most of the manuscripts of the original letter exchange remained in Arnim's family and was sold in 1929 to an American collector, Daniel Heineman. It is now held in the Heineman Collection at the Pierpont Morgan Library in New York (*BA* 1107–10). In addition to the large collection at the Morgan Library, several manuscript letters belong to the Goethe-Schiller Archive in Weimar, and a few became part of the Varnhagen Collection, now in Cracow. Surviving evidence suggests that Arnim occasionally made gifts of her manuscript letters and that a small number of these are now lost (*BA* 1109).

Though most of the original letters from 1807–1832 have survived, Arnim's manuscript for the 1835 publication of the *Correspondence with a Child* was destroyed, and therefore editors must depend on the published first edition as a copy text. Arnim unaccountably made a gift of the manuscript to her school, the Ursuline Convent in Fritzlar, and the sisters promptly burnt the manuscript. A substantial number of draft pages from the English translation have survived. Arnim gave seventy-three pages of manuscript from her English translation with many annotations to Karl August Varnhagen. These pages joined the large collection of Rahel Varnhagen's manuscripts, entering the Prussian Staatsbibliothek in Berlin, disappearing during the Second World War, and reappearing in the Jagiellonian Library in Cracow in 1977. A four-page draft of the English preface also survives in the Freies Deutsches Hochstift Collection in Frankfurt.

Goethe's Correspondence with a Child

Bettina von Arnim's 1835 *Goethe's Correspondence with a Child* is the best-known of the works in this study. Her work was popular in her lifetime and is currently undergoing a renaissance of interest among feminist literary critics. What I hope to do in this chapter is show how central the theme of female self-definition is to the book. This may seem paradoxical since the traditional reception of the book, brought to the attention of English-speaking readers in Milan Kundera's 1991 novel, *Immortality*, is that it is a book about Goethe, and that Arnim is little more than an opportunistic inside biographer, wishing to bathe in the light of his celebrity. Certainly, Arnim's work presents a laudatory portrait of Goethe (Joeres, "We are adjacent" 48 and Kelling 73–82). But what generations of critics have failed to see is how central to the work is the theme of a young woman's creativity and self-discovery. Reading the work from this perspective, one sees that admiration for the great poet is a means the author uses to present herself as the poet's soul-mate, and, ultimately, his peer. More than the literary monument that the subtitle suggests, Arnim's work is an act of expropriation and self-celebration.

Goethe's Correspondence with a Child, Bettina von Arnim's best-known book, is a strange hybrid of historical biography and epistolary novel. The bulk of the original letter exchange took place in the years 1807 to 1811, but after Goethe's death in 1832, prior to publishing the exchange in 1835, Arnim revised the entire exchange substantially, mostly augmenting her own letters, but also making some changes in Goethe's. The work that Arnim published in 1835, while appearing to be a historical letter exchange, was essentially a work of the imagination. Consider a typical passage from the book. In one sense, this passage raises the philological question of when it was written, whether in one of the letters of 1808 Arnim sent to Goethe, or whether part or all derived from Arnim's 1835 revisioning, following Goethe's death.

> Since I have loved you, something unattainable lingers in my spirit; a mystery that nourishes me. As the ripe fruits fall from the tree, so musings fall to me, to refresh and invigorate me. O Goethe! If the fountain had a soul, it could not rush with more anticipation toward the light than I with confidence hasten to meet the new life, which has been given to me through you .... (*BA* 2: 132)

But answering the historical question about the dates of the drafts seems to miss the point of the passage: it is a poetic utterance on the nature of love. More specifically, it is Arnim's epistolary contribution to her generation's discussion of poetry's inspirational sources. The Goethean influences manifest themselves in the choice of tropes and diction, but not in the syntax, nor the tone, and especially not in the nuances of emphasis and meaning. The Goethe addressed in this letter is as much an idealized figure of rarefied and transcendent love instead of the flesh and blood person with whom Arnim corresponded. Arnim's image of the spring evokes the passionate spirit of Solomon's love in the biblical *Song of Songs*. Her beloved is a mystery, a fountain, a source of new life in herself. The letter is a timeless rhapsody addressed to the embodiment of the spirit of love.

The central subject of Arnim's *Goethe's Correspondence with a Child* is love — aesthetic, idealized, Romantic love. While Goethe is certainly the focus of this love, he is not, by and large, its sole source. The letters from Goethe are for the most part playful and flirtatious, but briefer and much more restrained than Arnim's. They are not particularly memorable love letters, Arnim's redactions notwithstanding. There is no doubt that they are motivated by a genuine and complicated affection, but the overwhelming passion in the exchange comes not from Goethe but from Arnim. She speaks of love transfiguring her into a priestess (*BA* 2: 363, 451). Arnim's book proclaims ultimately a direct analogy between its own idea of Romantic love and the miraculous metamorphoses of the word becoming flesh, and the flesh, spirit:

> This flesh is become spirit.
> I have selected these words as an inscription for the monument. The lover's call to you, Goethe, will not remain unanswered. You enlighten, you elate, you permeate, you make perceptible, so the Word takes on flesh in the loving heart . . . . — Love does everything for love's sake, and the lover forsakes himself, devoting himself to love. (*BA* 2: 570–571)

These words were not ultimately inscribed by a sculptor on a monument of stone, as Arnim literally proposed, but on the last pages of the monument of correspondence by Arnim herself. Love, in her conception, can animate unknown energy in another and can thus transfigure. So, while it is true that the book is a literary monument to Goethe, it is Arnim's monument. Goethe is the object of her passion, but the great passion that fills the pages of the book is Arnim's.

Arnim's love letters are, if anything, more ethereal and spiritual than a traditional love lyric, because, unlike the traditional poetic lover, she is almost entirely uninterested in any of her beloved's physical qualities. Although there is no small erotic undercurrent in the correspondence, the eroticism is rarely sensual or physical. She does not catalogue the beauties of his features or imagine physical consummation of her love. Nor is she interested in the details of his social self or of his literary works. Goethe, in the letters, serves as the inspiration for a series of reflections on the profound, inspirational nature of love. One does not read Arnim's letters for a detailed critique of Goethe's writings. It is his soul she is in love with, a soul that could be that of any or all poets, not just the particular one who replied to her letters.

It is for this reason that I make the paradoxical claim that the central concern of *Goethe's Correspondence with a Child* is not the exchange between an eponymous Goethe and a child; rather, the dominant concern is the development of Arnim's own creative self. Like the beloved of a Petrarchan sonnet sequence, Goethe serves as the topic enabling the lover, Arnim to display her own immense powers of expression and to discover her identity as an artist.

Gender, Propriety, and Women's Writing

Anyone who doubts the difficulty faced by a woman with literary talent in bringing her work to print in Germany in the Romantic period should read the letter Clemens Brentano wrote to Arnim, his sister, upon learning that she intended to publish her correspondence with Goethe. Her book and its impending publication inspired Brentano to renew contact with Arnim after a long hiatus. Some passages were written before, some during, and some after the actual publication of *Goethe's Correspondence with a Child* in two parts in 1834 and 1835. In this long and important letter concerning her most renowned work, Clemens Brentano urges her to retract the publication of *Goethe's Correspondence with a Child*.

> ... does it serve any purpose in the long run, if everybody in Europe knows that you cannot sit properly on a sofa but put yourself shamelessly on a man's lap and that he, not respecting the dignity of a poor, foolish girl, puts up with it, etc. — and the whole scene is so strangely sketched and disjointed that the reluctant reader is forced to fill it in? Well, I fear for your children, your sons who are abroad, in respectable positions, forced to uphold the honor of the family, who through insults, arising from these confidences, may be forced into quarrels and duels, your daughters may go astray or lose all respect for you. (Arnim, *Werke*, ed. Härtl, 1: 693)

Arnim's brother objected to his sister publishing her letters to Goethe — letters which were already on their way to becoming one of the major literary works in the tradition of German women's writing — on the grounds of propriety. He condemned the work because he considers it immodest for a woman, young and unmarried at the time of the exchange, to engage in such intimacy and professions of love with a middle-aged poet. He saw it as presumptuous for Arnim to present her letters as literary works deserving of a public audience, as anything more than ephemeral private communications. He could not imagine her letters placed side-by-side with the letters of the great Goethe as if they were worthy of equal consideration. Although we may smile at Brentano's prejudices against his sister's literary ambitions, his criticism points out exactly what is bold and ambitious about Arnim's project. It is one thing for a young man to write love lyrics but quite another for a woman from a good family to attempt the same. Propriety will not suffer it.

In this long, important letter concerning the publication of *Goethe's Correspondence with a Child*, Clemens Brentano suggestively informs his sister that he is dissatisfied with Goethe's conclusion to *Faust II*. He writes: "I don't know to what extent you are satisfied with the conclusion of Goethe's *Faust*, history tells of a different end for this Faust . . . !" (Brentano 2: 336–40). Brentano brings up the subject of Goethe's seemingly idiosyncratic redemption of the sinner Heinrich Faust as the crux of his criticism of Arnim's book. Brentano prefaces his criticism by recounting the recent deaths of three people whom his sister loved: her husband Achim von Arnim in 1831, Goethe in 1832, and Friedrich Schleiermacher in 1834 — not only beloved to Arnim but to all significant contributors to literary Romanticism. After Brentano states the list, he contrasts their mournfully unjust departures with Faust's comparably unjustified apotheosis. Faust achieves legendary immortality while Achim von Arnim, Goethe, and Schleiermacher experienced human mortality. Brentano would have Arnim reverse Goethe's motion: where Goethe figuratively eternalizes his hero, she should literally snuff hers out. He would have her silence her love forever by suppressing the publication of her book.

The harshness of Brentano's censure of his sister's literary ambitions is further underlined by knowledge that before he knew she intended to publish it to the world, he had approved of her relationship with Goethe and looked forward to the biographical work she once planned to write.

> Goethe's conversations with Bettina are a treasure for us friends, he was like a child; he confessed to her that he often was grumpy and cold, that he wished her always near him, that then he would never grow old, that he had never loved a youth as quickly as he did you, that she could stay near him. He gave her permission to record his life as related by his mother. He said he would tell her much more on the subject, it would become his biography, simple like "The Children of Haimon." She behaved with him the way the Spirit speaks to the poet in *Hans Sachs*. She scolded him, encouraged him, improved him, and rejuvenated him in a matter of hours, and everything about him was just as we thought. As for the biography, keep it quiet! The book will be divine! (Clemens Brentano to Achim von Arnim, 17 Jul. 1807; Arnim, *Werke*, ed. Härtl, 1: 638)

Brentano was once so enthusiastic for his sister's "divine" Goethe book that even the conservative outlook he adopted in his mature years does not explain his harsh criticism of his sister when she actually published her letters. Clearly he had not imagined that his sister would be such an active figure in the book. He had imagined a literary, playful, yet polite biography as related by Goethe's mother, and not the record of overflowing youthful rapture that his sister actually produced. It was precisely the prominence in Arnim's books of her own actions and emotions that gave her brother so much offense, her freedom from social stricture that he found so threatening to decorum and his family's honor.

Furthermore, Brentano's urge to suppress his sister's creativity may help us to understand the logic behind Arnim's strategy of self-publication. She knew that the reading public was unlikely to take seriously the creative aspirations of a woman like herself. But she also knew the substantial public interest in Goethe and fascination the reading public would find in the confidential account of one of the great poet's intimate acquaintances. If she had wished to publish her own writing, she might never have found a printer. By focusing the work on Goethe, she guaranteed herself an audience she might never have otherwise had. In fact, if this was Arnim's strategy, it was successful, because the fame she gained from *Goethe's Correspondence with a Child* did enable her in subsequent years to publish her own work independently for a large audience. We have seen that each of the three women in this study believed or were instructed that it was improper to seek a public audience for their private letters. Each devised her own strategy in response to these admonitions. Schlegel-Schelling chose anonymity, except among the small sympathetic audience that saw her letters in manuscript. Varnhagen solved the problem by waiting until after her death to have her letters published as her own. Arnim, alone, ignored the criticism and published works during her lifetime that were controversial and potentially damaging to her reputation. She did so because she was more ambitious than fearful of losing social respectability.

Contrary to her brother's immediate, paranoid, and personal reading, Arnim's text taps into the universal power of literature to eternalize, and then she applies that power to her original idea of the Romantic doctrine of love. Arnim interprets Romantic love as a spiritual force most powerfully exerted on the margins of relationships and best expressed in a work poised on the border between genres. Because the work does not reside entirely within a familiar generic category, critics from her brother on will always be able to argue that it is an improper and imperfect work. Conversely, defenders will be able to parry such objections armed with Arnim's epistolary artistry in portraying the loving self and with her publicly manifested professional ambition. Thus, she differs crucially from her grandmother La Roche, who was "denied the essential ingredient of modern 'authorship'" and Arnim incurs thereby both the "responsibility for its defects" and the "credit for its excellencies" (Woodmansee 108).

Arnim's active hand as editor reveals the conflicting impulses of self-effacement and self-publication that result from the clash between her literary aspirations and her fear that those aspirations will suffer censorship if openly revealed. *Goethe's Correspondence with a Child* was controversial, but it was never literally censored; on the contrary, it was widely read and praised. However, the Prussian authorities did actually attempt to suppress publication of her later political work, *Ilius Pamphiluis and Ambrosia* (Meyer-Hepner 146–49). *Goethe's Correspondence with a Child* erects a permanent memorial to the border between the skill of personal letters and the art of correspondence, to the marginal area between lived relationships and sublime love, and to the space between concrete experience and abstract transcendence.

Self-Fashioning and Women's Literature

Arnim, much more than either of the other women of letters, uses her personal letters as a vehicle for self-fashioning and self-publication that became a crucial event, not only in her own career, but in the history of writing by women in German. Her work stands apart because of the degree to which she selected and rewrote her own letters, transforming them from occasional personal messages into a crafted, unified literary work. She is also unique because she published her own letters herself, in her lifetime. She dates and signs her name to the dedication: "Let us stay congenial toward each other. August of 1834. Bettina v. Arnim" (*BA* 2: 13). The act of publishing and dedicating the book is an assertion of authority, one that Schlegel-Schelling and Varnhagen never committed. It is an insistence of a woman's potential to present herself before a literary public. Konrad Feilchenfeldt has pointed to the book's ground-breaking aspect:

> In 1835, when Bettine von Arnim published *Goethe's Correspondence with a Child*, the significance of her publication lay not so much in her relationship to Goethe, but rather in the literary establishment of a form of publication, which opened the door to the author's further publishing projects of this sort.... Bettina von Arnim's *Works*, which included her "epistolary novels," sanctioned the characteristics of the genre of *the letter*, already recognized when the individual novels appeared, a genre previously valued for its content but not form. She achieved such a literary recognition not because of a philologically exact reprinting of the text materials she had in front of her, but rather, on the contrary, because of a method of working, which brought her editions of personal letters closer to the genre of epistolary novel. Between Romanticism and Biedermeier, women's literature transformed the personal letter into a work of art — made it literary — and so experienced a breakthrough to the surface of the institution of literature.
>
> (*RV* 10: 76–77)

Notwithstanding the fact that isolated women had published letters before Varnhagen and Arnim, *Goethe's Correspondence with a Child* was a turning point in German literature. The novelty and success of Arnim's work among German readers gave a new prominence to women's writing. And, as Konrad Feilchenfeldt observes, women's private writing for the first time was perceived and respected as public literary art.

In the preface, Arnim portrays herself as the work's editor, as editor of her own and of Goethe's letters. She describes the activity she engaged in as an editor in the preface. The pride with which Arnim signed her name to her work as author, editor, and publisher were unprecedented (Goozé). While the authoritative voice of the dedication belongs to Arnim the editor, the preface immediately following it belongs to Arnim the epistolary author. Speaking as an author, she tries to anticipate her future readers' reception: "This book is for good people and not for the bad ones" (*BA* 2: 14). This opening remark is important because it shows her aware of the controversy that will arise from the intimate relationship chronicled in the letters that follow. Rather than fearing that readers will consider her immodest for harboring such love for the poet, she insists that if there is any immodesty it belongs to the hostile reader who cannot see the essential innocence of the relationship the letters portray. Through her introductory material, we can see Arnim artfully playing her audience's curiosity against its prejudices in an effort to overcome the inevitable objections her work will provoke. She quotes a letter from the nobleman managing Goethe's posthumous literary estate.

> [Chancellor von Müller wrote:] "give me any page from this, doubtless, most heart-warming correspondence; I will religiously preserve it, and not show it around, or let it be copied...." So, I have passed over in silence the request of Chancellor Müller, but have not ungratefully forgotten it; may the use I have made of it prove to him both my thanks and my justification. (*BA* 2: 15)

It was common in the period to indicate the disposition of the source letters. Some authors of epistolary novels purport to have found their bundle of letters in a piece of furniture. Arnim's reference is more complicated. By quoting the Chancellor's approving comments, she implies that a reader with refined tastes and a warm heart will find no offense in the letters' pages. The Chancellor suggests that she not show the letters around to too wide a public. While this might be taken as censure, in fact it piques the reader's curiosity by suggesting that the letters contain an intimate correspondence that hitherto only a select group of readers has been privileged to read. So the letters' controversial aspects become a source not of scandal but of public fascination. A further strategy to gain acceptance for her work is of course the association with Goethe. While Arnim was relatively unknown when she published her work, she could rely on Goethe's fame to gain an audience. A reader coming to her book expecting a volume of literary reminiscences or table-talk would be better disposed toward the work, and the presumed legitimacy of the subject would no doubt counter any discomfort at its subject matter. Rather than shying from the exposure of publication, we see Arnim manipulating the controversial reception of her letters so as to increase public interest in the letters and vastly increase the readership for a woman's personal writing.

Rather than the enormous, lifelong volume of Varnhagen's correspondence, Arnim selected a discrete portion of her letters that formed a unified whole, all focusing on the topic of love and her relationship with Goethe.

Arnim's historical letter exchanges with Goethe and with his mother fit into a compact period of time, spanning the years from 1807 to 1811. This practice in turn prepared the way for her later publications of portions of her correspondence: *Die Günderode* in 1840, *Clemens Brentanos Frühlingskranz* in 1844, and *Ilius Pamphilius und die Ambrosia* in 1848.

Arnim's correspondence follows in what is increasingly being seen as a female tradition (Brinker-Gabler, *Deutsche Literatur*.) However, the subject of the correspondence — poetry and love — mark an important development in the emergence of women's literature. Prior to Arnim, much of women's writing was either devoted to social correspondence or romantic fiction: two areas the age had sanctioned as appropriate female topics of discourse. The correspondence of Caroline Schlegel-Schelling follows in the tradition of female predecessors, like the English letter-writer Montagu and the French letter-writer Sévigné. Arnim, an opponent of literary Philistinism and conventional taste (*BA* 2: 362 and 420), breaks away from established patterns of European women's writing. The female literary tradition, as unrecognized as it appears to us, was for Arnim perhaps too familiar — it belonged to the sentimental and illustrious past of her grandmother and foster mother Sophie von La Roche. Her presentation of love as a powerful force that a young woman can know through transcending her ordinary experiences of natural phenomena represents a Romantic revisioning of La Roche's female protagonist's search for socially-acceptable sentimentality. *Goethe's Correspondence with a Child* marks a decisive moment in the feminist reading of the history of German literature because it attempts to move beyond the sort of female tradition that La Roche's novels represent. The author's fascination with Goethe and her invocation of his name and privileged entitlement — literally as the first word of the title — represent a gesture of rupturing literary traditions. Arnim's book achieves the rupture in two ways; first, it invokes the name of a great, recognized poet, whose reputation at the time of publication was firmly established, and then it couples that name with her own; second, publishing her letters alongside with Goethe's suggests her ambition to have her work read alongside with that of the great poet, to be compared with it, and attributed the same respect. It is a calculated effort to break down the distinctions between the kinds of literary activity permitted to women and those permitted to men. In a compromise that ultimately contributes to breaking down the barriers restraining women's literature, Arnim adopts some of the formal conventions of traditionally male literary works, while simultaneously refusing to compromise on other structural and thematic issues, such as the inclusion of the long diary and the scenes of rapture and imagination.

Goethe's Correspondence with a Child evinces a complex pattern of formal structure. Arnim introduces the letters in a dedication and preface, followed by the letter exchange and diary and diverse insets: poems, travel narratives, and humorous excursions, within the letters, and anecdotes, exposition, and aphorisms, within the diary. Generic diversity complicates the formal unity of the published work. The internal anatomy of *Goethe's Correspondence with a Child* is not composed of the same integral parts as its superficial headings display. The book has five headings: 1) a Dedication to the Prince Pückler-Muskau, 2) a Foreword directed to the reader, 3) The First Part, 4) The Second Part, and 5) a Diary: Book of Love. Under the headings is a variety of text types: epistolary, diaristic, aphoristic, narrative, essayistic, and lyric (Waldstein, *Politics* 47). Three major pieces stand under Part I: the letters to Goethe's mother, the narrative on Günderrode, and letters to and from Goethe. The structure she gave the book — whether the result of her activity as author or as editor — challenges its readers to understand its order, design, and presentation and ultimately to relate its complex structure and development to its theme of the power of transcendent experiences of love.

Arnim's work can be best understood within the multivariate formal boundaries of the correspondence genre. Like Varnhagen, in the spirit of Romantic innovation, Arnim uses the work to experiment not only with the letter form but with several others. The work is structurally unique. Two prefatory texts precede it; the letters begin with the correspondence with Goethe's mother that led to the exchange with Goethe; then the author presents a series of reminiscences of wandering on the shores of the Rhine and of the recent suicide of the poet Karoline von Günderrode. Only then does she return to the correspondence in the title — its longest section. It concludes with an extensive section similar in content to many of the letters, but written as a diary. Thus, it appears to be original in both form and content. The result of this variety of forms is to counter the sense of linear plot and replace it with an organic structure in which themes appear and then are augmented and varied into a multiplicity of expressions.

One perhaps confusing aspect of the structure Arnim imposed on her correspondence is the large amount of apparently miscellaneous material intervening between the book's title page and the letters exchanged with Goethe. In addition to the introductory materials, a considerable number of pages in the first part are devoted to Arnim's correspondence with Goethe's mother, Elisabeth Textor Goethe, and to Arnim's reminiscences of the suicide of her friend, the remarkable poet, Karoline von Günderrode. Although the introductory material relating to Goethe's mother and Günderrode seem miscellaneous, they in fact serve some important purposes. What they have in common is that they introduce two different examples of female creative power, which, although not in any way threatening to Goethe's authority as poet, put it in a context, and make it clear that there are alternative kinds of generative authority.

The correspondence with Goethe's mother was of course historically Arnim's entree to society with Goethe himself. But while Arnim could easily have omitted it from the book, I believe she kept it because it introduces Goethe in a way that is unexpected and serves her purposes. One is used to thinking of Goethe as a lofty individual, standing apart from society, wrestling with his personal creative angels. He had become a peerless, cultural titan in the decades following Arnim's historical correspondence with him. To encounter him, then, as his mother's son is demystifying and more than a little comic. In contrast to the dignified picture we have of Goethe, his mother is chatty, folksy, gregarious, and not at all intimidated by her son's great accomplishments. Elisabeth Goethe was known as a raconteur, not an intellectual or cultural figure. She takes to Arnim because she recognizes in her a kindred spirit, a fellow woman distinguished by her lively graces and her power to knit together the community.

Arnim, who might not have been able to gain access to Goethe's society on her own, uses her conversational talents to approach him through his mother, and she makes no secret of the fact that Goethe's mother has used her maternal authority over her son to sanction the introduction. Goethe's mother abetted the young Arnim's love and admiration for her son, and encouraged her project of writing the eminent poet's biography. The thematizing of maternal power is quite blatant when Arnim proudly asserts that Elisabeth Goethe has declared her a spiritual daughter. "Dear — dear daughter! In the future call me by the name of mother, which is so dear to me . . . for that is really my role, where I am an expert" (Oehlke 5: 7). In quoting this letter to Goethe, Arnim focuses on the consequence of her generous invitation to filiation, which permits her a very special sibling relationship with the great master. She also stresses the duration of that relationship: Arnim may now claim to be writing to her "brother":

To Goethe.

Kassel, May 15th, 1807

"Dear, dear daughter! Call me always and forever by that one name that embraces my happiness. Let my son be your friend, your brother, who surely loves you," etc.

Goethe's mother writes such words to me; what right do they give me? It's as if a dam has broken within my heart . . .

So what shall I do? — tell how the glorious companionship you offered me, now flourishes in my heart, — all other life at once repressed? —

how I must ever yearn toward that time, when I first felt myself happy? All this is profitless; — the words of your mother! (*BA* 2: 86)

The words Goethe's mother writes inspire Arnim to a familial intimacy; they pave the way for the personal "Du" form; and they enable her to take a form of fraternal love for granted. And they create an ironic frame to the theme of Goethe's power as a poetic master. Elisabeth Goethe has a maternal social power over her son that transcends his own exalted cultural station. Arnim approaches him through his mother because she seeks a related form of power over him, the power, not just of a confidante or a biographer, but of a lover.

Seen in this light, there is an underlying logic to the apparent digression on Karoline von Günderrode that follows the correspondence with Goethe's mother yet intervenes before the correspondence with Goethe. Rather than a digression, it reads as an anticipatory echo for Arnim's central concerns. Günderrode was a woman poet, largely unrecognized in her own time. She was an intimate friend of Arnim's, and Arnim was devastated by her suicide in 1806, months before the start of the Goethe correspondence. Recounting Günderrode's tragic demise immediately prior to the meeting with Goethe suggests a powerful contrast for the attentive reader between the contemporary status of female and male poets: the one, obscure, and suffering premature death at her own hands, the other, comfortable and successful. More centrally, the section on Günderrode indicates that Arnim's passionate admiration of Goethe is just one kind of sublime love she was familiar with. It reminds the reader that female friendships may be equally passionate and elevated. We know that Arnim went on to publish a separate volume of her correspondence with Günderrode, whose reception was aided by the renown of the Goethe book. So in her book about the author of *Faust*, she was quietly preparing an audience that would be sympathetic to a work devoted exclusively to themes of female friendship and creativity, and she was anticipating the connection between impassioned love and aesthetic inspiration.

We have already seen that Varnhagen's book intentionally crafted the correspondence in order to present it as a literary work, going so far as to change several letters into the format of a diary. Arnim's revision of her original correspondence, however, went much further. Compared to other female letter-writers of the period, Arnim displays greater interest in the formal unity of her work. More than half of *Goethe's Correspondence with a Child* is a result of changes Arnim made after the historical correspondence of 1807–32. Vordtriede describes her process of composition: "Bettina works by interpolation. The texts get longer and longer in the manner of a baroque growth, until finally the second version of the original draft ends up somewhere in the back of the last draft, and the same happens with the third and fourth draft, and so on" (Vordtriede 76). She greatly expanded upon her own letters and embellished some of Goethe's seventeen letters, creating the impression of a greater degree of intimacy than that conveyed by Goethe's original letters.

For many decades after the book's publication, some readers and critics assumed that it contained the accurate historical letters exchanged between Arnim and Goethe. When it was discovered that she did in fact rewrite many of the letters, including Goethe's, many critics with some justification felt that Arnim had falsified her book. In this study, I am interested in the correspondence as a work of the imagination, not as a historical document. From my point of view, it is clear that Arnim rewrote the letters because she felt they could be improved. Her whole admiration for Goethe always had a timeless quality to it. Her actual social relationship with him was rather brief. And, in spite of Clemens Brentano's statements about the impropriety of their intimacy, most critics agree that they never physically consummated their love. Instead it was a love expressed largely in the pages of their letters, and the love expressed there is ethereal, abstract, and virtually Platonic. It is a love that rarely considers the physical pleasures that might accompany spiritual communion. The Goethe whom Arnim admired was more a personification of Romantic ideals of love than the flesh and blood poet. In this sense, whether Arnim wrote passages in 1804 or 1834 makes little difference. From our perspective the rewriting of the letters is comparable to the common poetic practice of rewriting and republishing early poetry, constantly seeking improvement.

Although she did not publicly confess to her rewriting of Goethe's letters, the act suggests her irrepressible desire not only to be read alongside with Goethe, or paint his definitive portrait, but actually, surreptitiously to become him. She proves, if only to herself, that she can put words in Goethe's mouth, that she can speak for him, improve upon his letters. It is the reverse of the kind of textual expropriation suggested by Friedrich Schlegel when he proposed rewriting Caroline Schlegel-Schelling's letters. Here the unknown woman writer usurps the textual voice of the celebrated male, and Goethe becomes a character enlivened and animated in Arnim's imagination, a character for whom she writes dialogue, whose emotions she puts into poetic language, thereby claiming for herself his creative authority.

Arnim does more than just rewrite her letters. The consequence of her revisions further erases the letters' origins as a social correspondence and transforms them into an independent creative work. An important innovation in this direction is the extent to which she effaces her own social identity and creates an epistolary persona through whom to address Goethe. The Arnim who speaks in the letters is a self-created character, not demanding of the reader familiarity with any historical personage. In the correspondence, Arnim idealizes herself. She is not simply the twenty-three-year-old who began a correspondence with the famous poet. Arnim rewrites her early letters, improving upon her youthful self, making herself more passionate, more eloquent. The entire historical friendship undergoes a similar process of imaginative rewriting. In history, Arnim's friendship with Goethe was relatively brief and was cut short by the jealousy of Goethe's wife and Goethe's refusal to continue the correspondence. But in the literary work, all the dissension and acrimony of the historical friendship is effaced. In the book, there is never any break. No insurmountable jealousy or animosity ever enters the pages of the correspondence to cast a shadow upon the central passionate relationship. In the correspondence, Goethe never turns down Arnim's love. Letters that Goethe never received from Arnim are not excluded but take up a prominent position as the final rhapsodic diary that concludes the book. In a sense, the revisions are a wish-fulfillment, elaborating the daydreams that accompanied the imperfections of Arnim's experience; but such idealization is the essence of literary visioning. Arnim's textual recreation of her correspondence transforms a social relationship into an ideal one, into a literary monument.

As a collection of love letters by Goethe, the book is disappointing. As Arnim's correspondent, he enters the book as less than her equal, a point underscored by the brevity and relatively small number of letters from him. Not only do her letters outnumber his, but they overpower his in sentiment and force of expression. Finally, his correspondence dwindles away. In the third section of the work, Arnim continues to write to him even after she has informed the reader of his death. But rather than bringing an end to her expressions of love or changing it to tones of mourning, the death of Goethe frees the narrative to achieve its least restrained and most ambitious celebrations of love's enduring reality. Although all this emotion is directed toward Goethe, its source is Arnim. And the drama of the work lies not in the life of its subject but in the growing powers of expression of its central author.

If Arnim idealizes her relationship with Goethe, she also idealizes her own identity. This self-recreation begins on the title page. The title clearly states that the book contains a correspondence of Goethe, yet it indicates neither the name nor the sex of the correspondent, referring to his correspondent simply as a *child*. Further into the book, it is clear that the *child* of the title is Bettina von Arnim. She signs the introduction to the book, and the letters are frequently also signed, *Bettina*. So, she does not omit her name from the title out of a desire for anonymity or a fear of publicity. Rather, the child is a persona that she creates for herself, one that frees her from her literal identity and allows her to play a role appropriate to her imaginative vision of herself. Arnim was in her twenties when she exchanged letters with Goethe — hardly a child — and she was in her fifties when she rewrote and titled the correspondence. Early on in her life, well before the composition of the original letters, let alone the first draft of the book, which was not written until the early 1830s, Bettina von Arnim first developed the voice of the child. She created the voice of the child in writing to her brother Clemens, a formative experience for her. What the early voice of the child has in common with the later, developed persona of the child is retrospect. Both versions look backward, back toward a golden age of innocence, and both seek a vision of harmony, engendered by love, not authority (Milch 74–77).

Arnim extols the absence of learning as a virtue. In contrast, Varnhagen deplores ignorance in herself and any others in whom the potential for education can be found; nevertheless, her situation as author is analogous to Arnim's. Arnim extols a child-like absence of learning because she chooses to construe childhood as a privileged and unsullied state, in which free-thinking, free-speaking, and free-form writing are not weakness but rather virtues. The author uses these virtues, moreover, as a privileged vantage from which she can view her construction of the character of the poet.

She also calls herself a child because the term is gender neutral. It helps to free herself from the socialized role demanded of women in the period. A child can be androgynous and unrestrained by the rules of sexual propriety that govern adult behavior. Her playfulness and flirtatiousness which appeared immodest in a young woman, become amusing and delightful when the same behavior is attributed to a child. All her life, Arnim was a critic of social strictures. The persona she creates for herself in her book is of a Romantic child, free to wander uninhibited along the banks of the Rhine, free to imagine herself the lover of her country's great poet, free to become, herself, a grand and sublime poetic lover.

Romantic Love and Self-Visioning

Arnim's concept of love in her *Goethe's Correspondence with a Child* defines the emotion as an art — beautiful, supernatural, and otherworldly — a kind of art of love, she writes. At the same time, she speaks of love as accompanying ordinary yet powerful life experiences. "I have the desire to hear talk of love, the entire world speaks of it, and there is plenty hatched up about it in novels, but nothing that I'm fond of hearing" (*BA* 2: 251). Arnim brings together many experiences in the love she creates in *Goethe's Correspondence with a Child*. Experiences from her interactions with Elisabeth Goethe, Karoline von Günderrode, Clemens Brentano, and even the mother she barely knew merge into the love she directs toward an image of Goethe.

Arnim's poetic language has roots in the western tradition of love lyrics but at the same time she expands her vision of the emotion so that at times she seems, like one of the contemporary idealist philosophers, to be writing about a transcendent intellectual category. The passage below was written in 1838 exclusively for "The Diary of a Child," which is the third part of her English translation — better termed rendition — of the Goethe book.

> What I have lived, never parts from me; the more I confide in the Past, the more devoted I feel to the Present. — Love only passes through life to forth-bring itself into eternity . . . . That I love, is the real existence I awake in, when I am alone thinking of weaning and with me fly the Gods into this lonely pensiveness. (*Werke und Briefe*, ed. Konrad, 1: 762)

Consider the passage above in comparison to the quotation below, a sample from a historical letter written and sent in April of 1808:

> Lord, sometimes I know a kind of art that makes the love that quickly fills up my heart flow out to you even if only in my thoughts, but such a dream burst[s] forth like a swollen river over a dam, tells you how many thousand times the memory of you stirs up a powerful life in me that I never before knew. (*BA* 2: 601)

Again, Arnim shows her predilection for a philosophical discussion of love clothed in metaphorical terms: she defines love as a variety of art. This allies her with the Jena Romantics, especially with Schlegel-Schelling's brother-in-law Friedrich Schlegel who favored erasing the line between the personal and the public in literary enterprise. The next phrase of her text names both the personal — " . . . love that quickly fills up *my heart*" — and the public — "to spill over into *you*." In contrast to Schlegel-Schelling, who filled her letters with the language of social communication, Arnim displays an intellectual stamina and rigor in sustaining the same theme through the entire work. Her letter continues espousing a new concept of love. She uses an "unnatural" image of "nature" to impress the reader: "It might be difficult to embark upon a voyage to the sun, since you would be deterred by the experience that you will never reach it; — at such moments, experience is nothing to me . . . " (*BA* 2: 143). Love is an ideal, metaphysical force. Although humans may never expect to attain it, they nevertheless must eternally strive for it.

At the same time as her love is ideal, it is powerfully personified in the figure of Goethe as she creates him. She began construction of an image of the poet even during her first historical encounter with Goethe; small wonder that the meeting confirmed her expectations. She related her impressions of the meeting on 23 April 1807 to her brother Clemens, the very person who had insisted that she become familiar with Goethe:

> ... but he is really very correct and gentle, and also considerate, he certainly has the proper respect for human nature. Whoever stands before him without pretension, with honest love, must indeed feel comfortable with him.... I told him that I wanted to write his life story, this pleased him, he was outright encouraging about it.... Dear Clemens, whoever has seen him as I have but doesn't love him as I do is not deserving of his glance, and if the whole world does not recognize him, then Bettine will be the one to sing his praises with joy.... Oh, dear Clemens what really pleased me so much — I was so much at ease with him, he was like a playmate with me. (*Werke,* ed. Müller, 5: 176)

The feeling she conveys in observing that "he was like a playmate with me" is the feeling she sought to find before she met him that historic afternoon. She had already found Goethe's letters to her grandmother about her mother, Maximiliane von La Roche. Thus, from her brother and indirectly from her mother and grandmother, Arnim became something of an expert on the early Goethe — his works and his life from youth until approximately 1805. Her brother encouraged her to read Goethe's works, any and all of them; she was attracted and impressed most by works that he had written when he was close in age and spirit to her twenty-two years. And it was neither the poet of *Hermann und Dorothea* nor the dramatist of *Iphigenia in Tauris* and *Faust,* but the poet of "Mahomet's Song" and the author of *Wilhelm Meisters Lehrjahre* who fascinated her. Her Goethe was the early, most purely Romantic Goethe.

Although her conception of love may be an idealized one, the method with which she develops the theme in her work is not logical or in the manner of a philosophical treatise. Like the other correspondences, the central aesthetic structure of the work has nothing to do with logical or narrative progression but inheres rather in the drama of the inner self and the subject's developing consciousness of her own emotional power. In an article comparing Jane Austen to several little-known eighteenth-century female epistolary novelists, Spacks offers two solutions to the epistolary author's problem of sustaining a work without narrative continuity and suspense. The solution is that feeling takes the place of event.

> Both uses of letters — as repositories for story, as registers of feeling — bear directly on issues of plot: the artifice that creates stories out of happenings. Epistolary novels reinforce feeling as female vocation by substituting notations of emotion for other kinds of happening and by making feeling the cause for all effects in the outer as well as inner world. Feeling constitutes power rather than weakness, these works maintain.
>
> (Spacks, "Female Resources" 93)

Although I have already shown the way in which literary correspondences differ from epistolary novels, this is an apt account of the technique of discursive development that Arnim uses in her vision of her relationship to Goethe. Although there are a thousand minor occurrences that fill the letters in their correspondence, these are the accidental details of lived experience and do little in the way of providing the reader with an enthralling narrative. Instead it is the history of Arnim's feelings for Goethe, her developing inner life, and her evolving powers of expressing those feelings that provide the unifying thread to the letters.

Throughout the letters, Arnim dawdles indulgently on each point, creating the appearance of an author who refuses to mark what is most important. Despite the serpentine route of her discourse, it does mark a path toward presenting a cogent demonstration of her ideal of love. For example, Arnim places the death of Goethe's mother at the division between the first and second volumes, much as she introduced the first volume via Goethe's mother's epistolary invitation to honorary childhood. She emphasizes the division by concluding the last letter of volume one with the single-sentence paragraph — "I have the best news to report from Mother" — and by beginning the second with the retrospective simple past tense — "When I last wrote to you it was Summer, I was on the Rhine and traveled later with a cheerful group of friends and relatives on the water to Cologne" (*BA* 230–31). Arnim interrupts what sounds like the opening of a pleasant narrative to insert her epistolary agenda:

> ... when I came back, I spent the final days with your mother, while she was friendlier, and more cheerful than ever. On the day before her death, I was with her, kissed her hand and received her blessing in your name. Because I didn't forget you for a moment; I knew quite well, she would have been happy to leave me your best love as an inheritance. (*BA* 2: 231)

While Arnim seems to digress aimlessly from the mother's death to her love for Goethe or to biographical memories, the letter — taken as a whole — intertwines the three. It suggests a simultaneous experience of the many conflicting aspects of love: the affection between a young woman and an aged friend, the joyful experience of friends traveling in the countryside together, the grief at the loss of a loved one. All of these are parts of a greater emotion, and rather than considering them separately, Arnim experiences them as simultaneous and part of a larger whole.

Although love is often all-consuming in Arnim's work, she knows that the emotion does not always achieve such levels of intensity. Love can coexist with melancholy, jealousy, and even boredom. "Oh, just don't ask why I am starting a new page already, even if I don't have anything new to tell you? — I honestly don't know yet how I'll fill it up" (*BA* 2: 120). She explicitly thematizes the act of transferring the private feeling of love to the written form: "What should I write to you, when I'm sad and have nothing new and cheerful to say? I'd rather send you a blank page, instead of first filling it with letters" (*BA* 2: 130). This letter derives from one of Goethe's sonnets, "X. Sie kann nicht enden" (*BA* 2: 1004; Daley). Arnim intersperses her highest flights of emotion with letters that dwell on petty jealousy.

> I seldom see Schelling, there is something about him that makes me uncomfortable, and this something is his wife, who is trying to make me jealous of you, she corresponds with a certain Pauline G. from Jena, about whom she is constantly telling me, how very fond of her you are, what darling letters you write, etc., I listen and it makes me sick.... Oh, it really doesn't matter, I can't desire that you like me best, but no one should dare compare their love for you with mine. (*BA* 2: 255)

It does not give her pause that at times her love may be unrequited; at times the grandeur of the emotion may be forgotten amidst the mundane considerations of everyday life. Arnim's love is not merely sentimental. She demonstrates an awareness of the changing moods and complexity of love, a complexity that does not inhibit her boundless enthusiasm for the emotion.

In her *Goethe's Correspondence with a Child*, Bettina von Arnim endeavors to write letters that are mediators of shared sentiments between sympathetic souls, that play the role of "registers of feelings" (Spacks, "Resources"). The work is furthermore highly self-conscious. Arnim seldom loses awareness of the fact that she is writing letters and that her relationship to Goethe exists as much in these epistolary expressions as it does outside of the letters. Because letters metaphorically present the speaking organ of the writer, the addressee may get some satisfaction from kissing the letters as does Werther. In the first letter to Goethe in *Goethe's Correspondence with a Child*, Arnim commissions her letter neither to be her lips to speak to Goethe nor her hands to reach him but instead to be her eyes. In disagreement with the principle of epistolary conversation, she asks not that Goethe read in them her love for him but that she be able to read his eyes and to include his forgiving glance in her letter. "I wish I could finish my letter with a look into your eyes; I'd quickly draw out a pardon for my presumption, and enclose it; then I wouldn't be anxious about my childish prattle, which for me is very much in earnest" (*BA* 2: 87).

The quotation above deliberately plays with rhetorical tropes that are conventional in letter writing by calling attention to the notion that letters metonymically represent the letter writer. Throughout, Arnim's work is highly aware of itself as literary art. She plays as a virtuoso, showing off a series of self-conscious literary devices, including ironic and hyperbolic apostrophes of Goethe as recipient; excursuses into the fantastic; dramatic declarations of sentiment; and, last, a strange, unique mixture of anthropomorphic metaphors of nature and ecological metaphors of humanity. She draws from this list of devices in order to animate her letters. She wishes to instill them with a soul — which may or may not be mortal — whose most glorious capability is communion with a divine poetic spirit. In Arnim's terms, the proper name for the transcendent act of communion is love. As such, the soul is not sublimated in the transcendental act but the same as it ever was, free, perhaps even compelled, to repeat unending expressions of adoration and desire.

She endeavors to animate her letters because she hopes that the reader will, through the epistolary work, achieve the insight she attains in transcendent love for Goethe. This insight allows for a new vision of natural beauty and human nature. In this understanding, it is not surprising to find the author speaking in natural metaphors that are characteristically Romantic.

> We have a cold, wet April; I see it from your letter; — it's like a general rain; all the heavens overcast from start to finish; It's true, you possess the art of showing your feelings in brief forms and lines, and in what you leave unexpressed, the assurance steals into someone's heart, that she's not indifferent to you; yes, I believe it, that I'm precious to you, in spite of your cold letter .... (*BA* 2: 141–42)

This salutation constitutes only the beginning of Arnim's attempt to animate the letter. Here she employs artistic embellishment, a simile that reverses the expected pathetic fallacy: rather than call on weather to produce a tremendous rain storm in a moment of emotional upheaval or passion, rather than call upon nature to mirror and contextualize her sentiments, the author sees the human world mirroring nature. She makes demands of Goethe's letter. She demands that it show the same sentiments as her environment, even if she must therefore romanticize an unglamorous, common act of nature and even if she must derive her assurance from cold silence. She describes a letter she received from Goethe as if she were a weather reporter and his letter a natural phenomenon.

On one level, Arnim amorously corresponds with Goethe, writing for his eyes only. Another level, external to the narrative, counters the character's gesture of privacy. She writes her letters as a private expression to her correspondent Goethe, but she writes letters that are also intended for a much wider public. Both an attention to private communication and public poetic rhetoric are evident in the passage quoted above. Seen from an external perspective, the author Arnim writes for readers, a plural number, expecting the letter's readers to exceed recipients. She typically supplies an interpretation of her own tropes — much as a map provides a legend. If Goethe were the only anticipated reader, then Arnim would be insulting his intelligence, and she would be overdetermining the meaning of the letter's beginning. Other readers however need the legend. Thus, she tells any outside readers that she is using vocabulary more commonly used to describe the sky and atmosphere — "overcast" and "cold, wet" — to portray Goethe's affection toward her. This self-interpreting passage (composed of one part metaphor, two parts explication) stands at the beginning of the letter and contains information that is helpful to marginal readers (figuratively marginal: namely those who are not addressed). The prevailing metaphor of the weather, its pathos and eros, gives this letter a lyrical tone and a sense of unity. The passage expresses Arnim's contrary and self-conscious love for the poet. By committing her love to paper, she places it in a sphere that is both private and public. Private is the author's moment of writing it down, sealing it in an envelope, and imagining the recipient receiving it. Public, however, is the journey the letter makes from sender to recipient; also public is the act of the recipient who opens a letter to other readers and the author's act of becoming her own editor and publisher.

Arnim writes of the most overwhelming love in the section that she published as the third and final part of her book, titled simply "Das Tagebuch," "The Diary." The diary is less coupled to concrete events than the preceding sections, and it becomes the locus for her most ambitious anthems to love. Although historians agree that she kept a diary from 1807 to 1811, at the same time as she exchanged letters with Goethe, and for some time thereafter, she composed the "Diary," the third section of *Goethe's Correspondence with a Child*, after Goethe's death.

Love and images of love in nature often serve Arnim in the diary because they illustrate her concept of intensification through repetition: . "My thoughts swarm around you like bees around a tree in bloom. They touch upon a thousand blossoms and leave one to visit the next, each one is new to them; so, too, love repeats itself, and each repetition is new to love" (*BA* 2: 319). Although love permeates everyday experience, it is ultimately and in its purest form an ahistorical force. It is a force that connects the characters. In the correspondence, Arnim writes to the poet of a celestial love that escapes all parameters of time: "Love is forever newborn, it is eternally a single moment, time is nothing to it, it is not in time, because it is eternal; Love is brief. Eternity is a heavenly briefness" (*BA* 2: 319). Love has no past. Her conception of love places it in a meta-chronological realm and motivates the book's narrative in a plethora of similes comparing eternal, heavenly love to miraculous acts of nature. She writes neither to communicate with her correspondent, nor to instruct him on her views, but rather to have a suitable backdrop for a woman to engage in written speculation.

Arnim maintains that love is more than a description of a personal relationship; it is an intellectual category. Love ultimately exists on a sublime level connected to abstract Christian sentiments; however, it is deeply rooted in the sensual. "I was born to serve in the temple..." (*BA* 2: 449) — the temple of Romantic love. Her correspondence with Goethe — her published epistolary novel and her original letters — burst with exclamations of overwhelming, vertiginous, quasi-religious, and quasi-erotic love.

Reviewing the structure of the book again finds that it initially uses the exchange with Goethe's mother to explore the nature of filial love, while with the narrative on the suicide of Karoline von Günderrode it elaborates on passionate friendship as an alternate variety of love. The central letter exchange with Goethe becomes a vehicle to express the highest form of inspirational love, which is made up in part of Arnim's devotion to the great poet but in essence of her devotion to poetic expression itself which finds its fullest voice in the climactic diary. Taken together, this work of correspondence depicts the boundless possibilities of the epistolary self; the self of this correspondence takes ordinary experiences and transcends them through the power of eternal love.

We have seen the paradoxical truth that Arnim's monument to Goethe is, centrally, a monument to herself. Arnim's love letters are a virtuoso performance in which she demonstrates the profundity and immensity of her emotion, not just to her beloved but to the world. She strives to possess Goethe, not just amorously, but creatively, as his sister in the craft of poetry. Yet, with relentlessly impassioned language, she shows her "good readers" the goal of her striving. She yearns to make him *her* Goethe. She wants her idea of him to be definitive. The underlying motive is not selfless admiration but an ardor that exalts the lover as well as the beloved. Arnim wishes in her letters to demonstrate to the world that she possesses a passion equal to, if not exceeding, that of the age's most celebrated poet. In so doing, she discovers her own identity as an artist.

Conclusion:
The Self in Context

> *To prevent an inner life that has no useful purpose from sinking into nothingness, to assert herself against given conditions which she bears rebelliously, to create a world other than that in which she fails to attain her being, she must resort to* self-expression. *Then, too it is well known that she is a chatterer and a scribbler; she unbosoms herself in conversations, in letters, in intimate diaries.*
>
> (Beauvoir 783)

When trying to summarize these works as a critic, it is tempting to fall back on generalizations about the women's lives and the periods they lived in. These generalizations, however, tend to place the women's private lives in the context of a public world that never fully appreciated their creativity. And so, by summarizing, we run the danger of losing sight of the specificity and complexity of these women's personal experiences and thereby diminishing them. The women's inner lives had their own dynamics, often quite distinct from what was happening in the public sphere of their marriages, friendships, and social lives. What is most difficult is to be true to the actual lived drama of these women's inner lives. Nothing can convey the literary selves these women constructed so well as the actual correspondences.

Other difficulties arise when putting these women's lives in context. What we mean by context usually means our received account of the history of culture and society. Nancy K. Miller remarks on the difficulty of reading women's lives without including "the frame of *interpretations* that have been elaborated over generations of critical activity" (*Subject* 129). Carolyn Heilbrun warns that when we consider women's lives against the background of our received account of context, we may be putting them in a framework that is incommensurate with the complexity and authenticity of their experience (*Writing* 18–19). Heilbrun wishes that she as a young reader had had women's lives to read; my generation is making not only the accounts of women's lives available but is also striving both to produce the frameworks of interpretation she finds lacking and to elaborate a critical appreciation of those women's writings. I hope that this book and the work of a new generation of scholars will lead to a shared understanding of literary self-expression in the past that takes account of women's creative struggles as letter writers.

Still another intriguing difficulty arises from including our three authors in a consideration of German Romanticism. Literary critics will have to reappraise some long-standing notions about the period. The Romantic period is commonly thought of as a time when authors challenged the literary traditions that had prevailed in the eighteenth century, rejected enlightenment strictures, questioned and generally explored emotional truths as opposed to rational ones. Some of these general notions, on the one hand, are borne out in the work of the three women. Schlegel-Schelling, Varnhagen, and Arnim were contemporaries and acquaintances of Friedrich Schlegel, Tieck, Goethe, Novalis, the brothers Grimm, and other representatives of Romanticism. Similarities of subject and perspective between men's and women's written works do exist, and sometimes the lines of influence cannot be untangled satisfactorily. On the other hand, none of our three authors is a woman attempting to write like a man. Reading their work suggests that the experience of the Romantic period was significantly different for women than it was for men. There are countless yet not always quantifiable ways in which these women's writing is uniquely female. These differences are not limited to the superficial aspects of gender. The women letter writers often write as if they inhabit different realms of experience. This difference is vividly apparent in the contrast between Goethe's and Arnim's letters in the *Correspondence with a Child*. Goethe's original letters are paternal, playful, but rather formal. Arnim, in contrast, takes the same experience and transforms it into passionate romantic fantasy. If the two sets of letters had been found separately, it might be hard to imagine that they were part of the same correspondence. There may be enormous categorical differences between women's writing and the writing of their male contemporaries. There is an entirely different perspective on the dialectic of private and public between men's writing and women's letters in the Romantic period. Even though Schlegel-Schelling may be as eloquent, although Varnhagen may be as ambitious, although Arnim may be as extroverted as a man of letters may be, it nevertheless often seems as if men were writing in a different genre with an entirely different relationship to conventions and rules of composition. Admittedly, men of the Romantic period wrote personal letters, some of them intimate, passionate, and self-fashioning. Nonetheless, it is true that the dialectic of public and private and the complex subordination of letters to literature conspired to impede women authors and that the impediment affects the female voice. I offer two examples. As a letter reader, I have encountered genuine modesty and jealousy in both men's and women's letters, yet I have found confident self-presentation and open competition only in men's letter writing. Similarly, while both male and female authors published personal letters in the nineteenth century and while I have encountered powerful writing in both genders, I have never encountered in women's letters the straightforward pride of empowerment that appears in young men who display their epistolary talents in public. Even Arnim who yearns most strongly for this empowerment must approach it surreptitiously and indirectly. Although I am as curious as any reader to locate the categorical differences between men's writing and women's writing, I am reluctant to draw many generalizations from my examples about the differences between men's writing and women's writing of the period except to say that they are different, that many of those differences are rooted in social constructions of gender, and that neglecting to respect the work of one sex or the other runs the risk of producing an incomplete view of the cultural experience of the past.

I hope I have provided a heuristic framework for reading the work of women who wrote letters in the two centuries prior to our own, and I hope with Carolyn Heilbrun that succeeding generations will continue to elaborate the critical frameworks that help us appreciate women's literary journeys of self-discovery. Many other German women in the period wrote important letters: Luise Gottsched, Henriette Herz, Dorothea Veit Schlegel, and Karoline von Günderrode, for instance. Lorely French's 1996 study gives many more examples of German women whose personal letters have survived. When scholars widen the scope to include correspondences by women written in other languages, the field becomes enormous. Many contemporary readers will have been unfamiliar with these correspondences. I have attempted to replace unfamiliarity with understanding for these historical works: a grasp of the generic problems distinct to women's correspondences, a series of readings of representative passages, and, most important, an appreciation for the way in which the women used the genre as a means of self-discovery and creative expression.

The preceding chapters have traced the appeal of the generic form to the aspirations and constrictions perceived by women artists. Correspondence was a central contemporary genre for women's extensive exploration of daily experience, familiar relationships, and social friendships. Although it is easy to see how they differ, qualities common to a literary genre are shared by the works of Schlegel-Schelling, Varnhagen, and Arnim; in their books, literary correspondence became a medium well-suited for the development and expression of artistic talent. The personal letter was a form they knew well and had practiced since girlhood. Even for most of their mothers' generation, the letter was accepted as a proper venue for communicating central personal concerns, for recording and considering private lives. Moreover, we have seen that each of these women writers arrived at a stage of epistolary maturity where she found the freedom to explore her private self, to develop a characteristic literary voice, and to attempt an unprecedented mixture of artistic forms.

In the hands of women of letters, correspondences were a versatile and viable medium for self-expression. For Caroline Schlegel-Schelling, the form allowed her to leave a record of her integrity as she struggled through her dramatic marriages, the tragic losses of a husband and children, the political turmoil of the Mainz Republicans, and the cultural and aesthetic revolutions of Romanticism. Although her life took place in the context of those events, it was not dependent on them but became an extended, personal struggle for equanimity. Rahel Varnhagen and Bettina von Arnim, each in her own unique way, took the form of the personal correspondence and used it for more ambitious self-expression. Varnhagen used her letters to express her grandiose, tragic sense of her own intelligence and personal identity as a Jewish woman. In her letters, egotism becomes a high art. Communication with her correspondent gives way to an assertion of her yearning for imaginative transcendence, a yearning invariably in conflict with her pervading emotion of pessimism. Arnim, the most publicly ambitious of these authors, uses her correspondence with Goethe as a means of imaginative self-vision. Her book is not ultimately an homage to Goethe so much as it is a virtuoso display of her immense poetic passion and urge toward self-creation. Through her letters, she creates a poetic rhapsody to the powers of Romantic love. What these three authors have in common is that their letters become an outlet for their urgent, insuppressible desire for expression.

Within the episodic, dialogic framework of correspondence, there can be no objective and absolute set of rules to categorize this provisional genre. Although each of these three correspondences creates in a sense its own generic rules, all three share in the act of creatively and actively giving expression to the self. Without ignoring their multiplicity, we can read the correspondences for the concern they share, which is inseparably linked to their formal presentations: that is the concern for the construction of a literary self. Personal letters, grouped into correspondences, enable and in fact necessitate an act of self-presentation and definition. Ordering letters in a series one after the other produces a delightful yet kaleidoscopic multiplicity. As readers of these works, we can never forget that they consist of letters sent out intermittently over a long duration, over a lifetime. So, we may find the self evolving in unexpected ways throughout the body of a correspondence, and, when the work's shape is defined by the arbitrary yet final closure of death, the evolution may strike the reader as incomplete; in Beauvoir's existentialist terms, the woman of letters "fails to attain her being" (783). However, despite pressures from social definitions of femininity, we have heard these works give voice to a dynamic and conflict-laden individuality.

For and against Beauvoir, I argue that the German women of letters did "traverse the given in search of its secret dimensions" (791). I see the correspondence form as an ingenious, provisional solution to the problem faced by women writers who want to search the given for an epiphany of brilliance yet whose "given" has in the past been labeled as inferior. Women of letters search for those secret dimensions of experience one installment at a time, in one letter succeeded by another, in response and self-response, and in revision and self-revision, until they have compiled a correspondence. At times unintentionally and elsewhere self-consciously, women of letters wrote to each other either to express their artistic identities in one half of a dialogue, or they wrote to discover such an identity in the dynamic process of creating an epistolary self. The literary identity of the writing and speaking self comes to maturity within the work of correspondence. The epistolary selves do not, however, remain static; instead, every successive reader participates in their ongoing and never perfected evolution. It is this act of gaining self-vision and sharing it that gives the three correspondences their coherence and their power. Only when we learn properly to read these letters from a past generation of women writers as imaginative accounts of self-discovery will their personal struggles for creative selfhood once again come to life.

Bibliography

Adelson, Leslie. "The Question of a Feminist Aesthetic and Karin Struck's *Klassenliebe*." Cocalis and Goodman 335–50.

Altman, Janet Gurkin. *Epistolarity: Approaches to a Form*. Columbus: Ohio State UP, 1982.

Arendt, Hannah. *Rahel Varnhagen: Lebensgeschichte einer deutschen Jüdin aus der Romantik*. 1959. Frankfurt: Ullstein, 1975.

——. *Rahel Varnhagen: The Life of a Jewess*. Trans. Richard and Clara Winston. London: East and West, 1957.

——. *Rahel Varnhagen: The Life of a Jewess*. Ed. Liliane Weissberg. Trans. Richard and Clara Winston. Baltimore, MD: Johns Hopkins UP, 1997.

Arnim, Bettina von (also cited as Bettine Brentano). *Goethe's Briefwechsel mit einem Kinde: Seinem Denkmal*. 3 vols. Berlin: Dümmler, 1835. Translated as *Goethe's Correspondence with a Child: For His Monument*. Trans. Bettina von Arnim et al. Berlin: Trowitzsch, 1837–38.

——. *Sämtliche Werke*. Ed. Waldemar Oehlke. 7 vols. Berlin: Propyläen, 1920–22.

——. *Werke*. Ed. Heinz Härtl. 2 vols. Berlin: Aufbau, 1986–89.

——. *Werke und Briefe*. Ed. Gustav Konrad. 5 vols. Vol. 5 ed. Joachim Müller. Frechen: Bartmann, 1959–63.

——. *Werke und Briefe*. Ed. Walter Schmitz and Sibylle von Steinsdorff. 3 vols. to date. Frankfurt: Deutscher Klassiker, 1986- .

Bakhtin, M. M. *The Dialogic Imagination: Four Essays*. Ed. Michael Holquist. Trans. Caryl Emerson and Michael Holquist. Austin: U of Texas P, 1981.

Barnouw, Dagmar. "Enlightenment, Identity, Transformation: Salomon Maimon and Rahel Varnhagen." *The German-Jewish Dialogue Reconsidered: A Symposium in Honor of George L. Mosse*. Ed. Klaus L. Berghahn. New York: Lang, 1996. 39–58.

Bäumer, Konstanze and Hartwig Schultz. *Bettina von Arnim*. Stuttgart: Metzler, 1995.

Bäumer, Gertrud, ed. *Goethes Freundinnen: Briefe zu ihrer Charakteristik*. Leipzig: Teubner, 1909.

Baym, Nina. *Woman's Fiction: A Guide to Novels by and about Women in America, 1820–70*. 2nd ed. Urbana: U of Illinois P, 1993.

Beauvoir, Simone de. *The Second Sex*. Trans. H. M. Parshley. New York: Vintage, 1974.

Becker, Heinz. "Die Briefausgabe als Dokumentenbiographie." Frühwald, Mähl, and Müller-Seidel 11–25.

Becker-Cantarino, Barbara, ed. *Die Frau von der Reformation zur Romantik: Die Situation der Frau vor dem Hintergrund der Literatur- und Sozialgeschichte.* Bonn: Bouvier, 1980.

———. "'Gender Censorship': On Literary Production in German Romanticism." *Women in German Yearbook: Feminist Studies in German Literature & Culture* 11 (1995): 81–97.

———. *Der lange Weg zur Mündigkeit: Frauen und Literatur in Deutschland von 1500 bis 1800.* Munich: Deutscher Taschenbuch, 1989.

———. "Leben als Text: Briefe als Ausdrucks- und Verständigungsmittel in der Briefkultur und Literatur des 18. Jahrhunderts." Gnüg and Möhrmann 83–103.

———. "Priesterin und Lichtbringerin: Zur Ideologie des weiblichen Charakters in der Frühromantik." Paulsen 111–24.

Behrens, Katja, ed. *Frauenbriefe der Romantik.* Frankfurt: Insel, 1981.

Benhabib, Seyla. "The Pariah and Her Shadow: Hannah Arendt's Biography of Rahel Varnhagen." *Feminist Interpretations of Hannah Arendt.* Ed. Bonnie Honig. University Park: Pennsylvania UP, 1995. 83–104.

Berdrow, Otto. *Frauenbilder aus der neueren Literaturgeschichte.* Stuttgart: Cotta, 1900.

———. "Rahel Levin, eine Vorkämpferin der modernen Frauenemanzipation." *Die Frau* 5.2 (1897): 108–16.

Beyer, Paul. "Bettinas Arbeit an 'Goethes Briefwechsel mit einem Kinde.'" *Von deutscher Sprache und Art: Beiträge zur Geschichte der neueren deutschen Sprache, zur Sprachkunst, Sprachpflege, und zur Volkskunde.* Ed. Max Preitz. Frankfurt: Diesterweg, 1925. 65–82.

Blackall, Eric A. *The Novels of the German Romantics.* Ithaca: Cornell UP, 1983.

Blackwell, Jeannine. "Anonym, verschollen, trivial: Methodological Hindrances in Researching German Women's Literature." *Women in German Yearbook: Feminist Studies and German Culture* 1 (1985): 39–59.

———. Introduction to "Bettina von Arnim." In Blackwell and Zantop, 445–49.

Blackwell, Jeannine, and Susanne Zantop, eds. *Bitter Healing: German Women Writers From 1700 to 1830: An Anthology.* Lincoln: U of Nebraska P, 1990.

Bohrer, Karl Heinz. *Der romantische Brief: Die Entstehung ästhetischer Subjektivität.* Munich: Hanser, 1987.

Böttger, Fritz. *Bettina von Arnim: Ein Leben zwischen Tag und Traum.* Berlin: Nation, 1986.

———, ed. *Frauen im Aufbruch: Frauenbriefe aus dem Vormärz und der Revolution von 1848.* Berlin: Nation, 1977.

Bovenschen, Silvia. *Die imaginierte Weiblichkeit: Exemplarische Untersuchungen zu kulturgeschichtlichen und literarischen Präsentationsformen des Weiblichen.* Frankfurt: Suhrkamp, 1979.

———. "Über die Frage: Gibt es eine 'weibliche' Ästhetik? — welche seit kurzem im Umlauf die feministischen Gemüter bewegt — gelegentlich auch umgewandelt in die Frage nach den Ursprüngen und Möglichkeiten weiblicher Kreativität." *Ästhetik und Kommunikation: Beiträge zur politischen Erziehung* 7.25 (1976): 60–75.

Brentano, Clemens. *Clemens Brentano: Briefe.* 2 vols. Ed. Friedrich Seebaß. Nuremberg: Karl, 1951.

Brentano, Peter Anton von. *Schattenzug der Ahnen der Dichtergeschwister Clemens und Bettina Brentano.* 1940. Bern: Lang, 1970.

Brinker-Gabler, Gisela. "Das weibliche Ich: Überlegungen zur Analyse von Werken weiblicher Autoren mit einem Beispiel aus dem 18. Jahrhundert: Sidonia Hedwig Zäunemann." Paulsen 55–65.

———. *Deutsche Dichterinnen vom 16. Jahrhundert bis zur Gegenwart.* Frankfurt: Fischer, 1978.

———, ed. *Deutsche Literatur von Frauen.* 2 vols. Munich: Beck, 1988.

Brockmeyer, Rainer. *Geschichte des deutschen Briefes von Gottsched bis zum Sturm und Drang.* Diss. U of Münster, 1961.

Brodhead, Richard. *Cultures of Letters: Scenes of Reading and Writing in Nineteenth-Century America.* Chicago: U of Chicago P, 1993.

Brun-Münter, Friederike. *Tagebuch einer Reise durch die östliche, südliche, und italienische Schweiz.* Zurich: 1800.

———. *Tagebuch über Rom.* 2 vols. Zurich: 1801.

Bürger, Christa. "Arbeit am Ich: Zu Rahel Varnhagens Schreibprojekt." *Merkur* 37 (1983): 116–21.

———. *Leben Schreiben: Die Klassik, die Romantik und der Ort der Frauen.* Stuttgart: Metzler, 1990.

Burger, Emil, ed. *Deutsche Frauenbriefe aus zwei Jahrhunderten.* Frankfurt: Diesterweg, 1908.

Burkhard, Marianne, ed. *Gestaltet und Gestaltend: Frauen in der deutschen Literatur.* Amsterdamer Beiträge zur neueren Germanistik 10. Amsterdam: Rodopi, 1980.

Carriere, Moriz. "Bettina von Arnim." *Lebensbilder.* Leipzig: Brockhaus, 1890. 226–75.

Cixous, Hélène. "Le rire de la méduse." *L'arc* (1975): 39–54. Translated as "The Laugh of the Medusa." Trans. Keith Cohen and Paula Cohen. *Signs* 1 (1976): 875–93.

Clauss, Elke. *Liebeskunst: Untersuchungen zum Liebesbrief im 18. Jahrhundert.* Stuttgart: Metzler, 1993.

Cocalis, Susan L., and Kay [Katherine R.] Goodman, eds. *Beyond the Eternal Feminine: Critical Essays on Women and German Literature.* Stuttgarter Arbeiten zur Germanistik 98. Stuttgart: Heinz, 1982.

Collins, Hildegard Platzer, and Philip Allison Shelley. "The Reception in England and America of Bettina von Arnim's *Goethe's Correspondence with a Child.*" *Crosscurrents* 2 (1962): 97–74.

Corngold, Stanley. *The Fate of the Self: German Writers and French Theory.* New York: Columbia UP, 1986.

Craig, Charlotte M. "Heritage and Elective Affinity: Bettina Arnim's Surrogate Mother and the Eternal Feminine." *Germanic Notes* 16.4 (1985): 54–57.

Craig, Gordon. *The Germans.* London: Pelican, 1982.

Culley, Margo. "Women's Vernacular Literature: Teaching the Mother Tongue." Hoffman and Culley 9–17.

Cutting-Gray, Joanne. "Hannah Arendt's Rahel Varnhagen." *Philosophy and Literature* 15 (1991): 229–45.

Daley, Margaretmary. "Corresponding Artists: Self and Genre in the Letters of Goethe, Schiller, Schlegel-Schelling, Varnhagen, and von Arnim." Diss. Yale U, 1994.

——. "Playing Charades with Goethe: The Identity of the Beloved in his 'Charade.'" *Seminar: A Journal of Germanic Studies* 33.2 (1997): 95–107.

Delilkhan, Rohith-Gerald. *Apologie der Briefkultur: Historische Geltung und hermeneutische Anforderungen der Briefe aus dem Gleimkreis.* Constance: Hartung-Gorre, 1991.

Derrida, Jacques. *Positions.* Trans. Alan Bass. Chicago: U of Chicago P, 1981.

——. *The Post Card: From Socrates to Freud and Beyond.* Trans. Alan Bass. Chicago: U of Chicago P, 1987.

——. "The Purveyor of Truth." Trans. Willis Domingo, et al. *Yale French Studies* 52 (1975): 31–113.

Dischner, Gisela. *Bettina von Arnim: Eine weibliche Sozialbiographie aus dem 19. Jahrhundert.* Berlin: Wagenbach, 1977.

——. *Caroline und der Jenaer Kreis: Ein Leben zwischen bürgerlicher Vereinzelung und romantischer Geselligkeit.* Berlin: Wagenbach, 1979.

——. "Die Romantikerin." *Emma* Dec. 1979: 50–55.

Donovan, Josephine, ed. *Feminist Literary Criticism: Explorations in Theory.* Lexington: UP of Kentucky, 1975.

Dotzler, Bernhard J. "'Seht doch wie ihr vor Eifer schäumet': Zum männlichen Diskurs über Weiblichkeit um 1800." *Jahrbuch der deutschen Schillergesellschaft* 30 (1986): 340–82.

Drewitz, Ingeborg. *Bettine von Arnim: Romantik — Revolution — Utopie.* Düsseldorf: Diederichs, 1969.

Duden, Barbara. "Das schöne Eigentum: Zur Herausbildung des bürgerlichen Frauenbildes an der Wende vom 18. zum 19. Jahrhundert." *Kursbuch 47: Frauen* (March 1977): 125–40.

Ellison, Julie. *Delicate Subjects: Romanticism, Gender, and the Ethics of Understanding.* Ithaca: Cornell UP, 1990.

Engelsing, Rolf. *Der Bürger als Leser: Lesergeschichte in Deutschland 1500–1800.* Stuttgart: Metzler, 1974.

Farrell, Michèle. "Sévigné: The Art of Vicarious Living." *Women in French Literature.* Stanford French and Italian Studies 58. Ed. Michel Guggenheim. Saratoga, CA: Anma Libri, 1988. 65–75.

Feilchenfeldt, Konrad. "Rahel Varnhagens Ruhm und Nachruhm." Varnhagen, *Gesammelte Werke* 10: 128–78.

——. "'Berliner Salon' und Briefkultur um 1800." *Der Deutschunterricht: Beiträge zu seiner Praxis und wissenschaftlichen Grundlegung* 36.4 (1984): 77–99.

Feilchenfeldt, Konrad, and Rahel E. Steiner. "Rahel Varnhagens 'Werke.'" Varnhagen, *Gesammelte Werke* 10: 75–127.

Frank, Erich. *Rezensionen über schöne Literatur von Schelling und Caroline in der Neuen Jenaischen Literatur-Zeitung.* Sitzungsberichte der Heidelberger Akademie der Wissenschaften 3. Heidelberg: Winter, 1912. 3–64.

Frederiksen, Elke P. "German Women Writers in the Nineteenth Century: Where are they?" Cocalis and Goodman 177–201.

——. "Heinrich Heine and Rahel Levin Varnhagen: Zur Beziehung und Differenz zweier Autoren im frühen 19. Jahrhundert: Mit einem unbekannten Manuskript von Heine." *Heine-Jahrbuch* 29 (1990): 9–38.

Frederiksen, Elke P., and Katherine R. Goodman. *Bettina Brentano-von Arnim: Gender and Politics.* Detroit: Wayne State UP, 1995.

Frederiksen, Elke, and Monika Shafi. "'Sich im Unbekannten suchen gehen': Bettina von Arnims 'Die Günderode' als weibliche Utopie." *Frauensprache — Frauenliteratur? Für und Wider einer Psychoanalyse literarischer Werke.* Ed. Inge Stephan and Carl Pietzcker. Kontroversen, alte und neue 6. Ed. Albrecht Schöne. Tübingen: Niemeyer, 1986. 54–61.

French, Lorely Elsa. "Bettine von Arnim: Toward a Women's Epistolary Aesthetics and Poetics." Diss. U of California, Los Angeles, 1986.

———. *German Women as Letter Writers: 1750–1850*. Madison: Fairleigh Dickinson, 1996.

———. "'Meine beiden Ichs': Confrontations with Language and Self in Letters by Early Nineteenth-Century Women." *Women in German Yearbook: Feminist Studies and German Culture* 5 (1989): 73–89.

Friedrichsmeyer, Sara. *The Androgyne in Early German Romanticism*. Bern: Lang, 1983.

———. "Caroline Schlegel-Schelling: 'A Good Woman, and No Heroine.'" Goodman and Waldstein 115–36.

Frühwald, Wolfgang, Hans-Joachim Mähl, and Walter Müller-Seidel, eds. *Probleme der Brief-Edition*. Kommission für germanistische Forschung: Mitteilung 2. Bonn: Deutsche Forschungsgemeinschaft, 1977.

Fuller, Margaret. *The Letters of Margaret Fuller*. Ed. Robert N. Hudspeth. 5 vols. Ithaca: Cornell UP, 1983–88.

Geiger, Ludwig. "Goethe, Bettine, und die Frankfurter Juden." *Allgemeine Zeitung des Judenthums* 67 (1903): 474–77.

Gellert, Christian F. *Werke*. Ed. Gottfried Honnefelder. 2 vols. Frankfurt: Insel, 1979.

Genette, Gérard. "Genres, 'types,' modes." *Poétique* 32 (1977): 407–421.

———. *Narrative Discourse*. Trans. Jane E. Lewin. Ithaca: Cornell UP, 1980.

Gersdorff, Dagmar von. *Bettina und Achim von Arnim: Eine fast romantische Ehe*. Berlin: Rowohlt, 1997.

Gilbert, Sandra M., and Susan Gubar. "Ceremonies of the Alphabet: Female Grandmatologies and the Female Authorgraph." *The Female Autograph: Theory and Practice of Autobiography from the Tenth to the Twentieth Century*. Ed. Domna C. Stanton. Chicago: U of Chicago P, 1984. 21–48.

———. *The Madwoman in the Attic: The Woman Writer and the Nineteenth-Century Literary Imagination*. New Haven: Yale UP, 1979.

Gnüg, Hiltrud, and Renate Möhrmann, eds. *Frauen-Literatur-Geschichte: Schreibende Frauen vom Mittelalter bis zur Gegenwart*. Stuttgart: Metzler, 1985.

Goethe, Johann Wolfgang. *Sämtliche Werke. Jubiläums Ausgabe*. 40 vols. Stuttgart: Cotta, 1940.

———. *Werke*. Ed. Erich Trunz. 14 vols. Hamburg: Wegner, 1948–60.

Goldsmith, Elizabeth C., ed. *Writing the Female Voice: Essays on Epistolary Literature*. Boston: Northeastern UP, 1989.

Goncourt, Edmond de, and Jules de Goncourt. *The Woman of the Eighteenth Century: Her Life, From Birth to Death, Her Love and Her Philosophy in the Worlds of Salon, Shop, and Street*. Trans. Jacques le Clerq and Ralph Roeder. London: Allen, 1928.

Goodman, Katherine R. "'The Butterfly and the Kiss': A Letter from Bettina von Arnim." *Women in German Yearbook: Feminist Studies in German Literature & Culture* 7 (1991): 65–78.

———. "The Impact of Rahel Varnhagen on Women in the Nineteenth Century." Burkhard 125–53.

———. *Dis / Closures: Women's Autobiography in Germany Between 1790 and 1914.* New York: Lang, 1986.

———. Introduction to "Rahel Varnhagen (1771–1833)." In Blackwell and Zantop, 403–07.

———. "Weibliche Autobiographien." Gnüg and Möhrmann 289–99.

Goodman, Katherine R., and Edith Waldstein, eds. *In the Shadow of Olympus: German Women Writers around 1800.* Albany: State U of New York P, 1992.

Goozé, Marjanne Elain. "Bettina von Arnim, the Writer." Diss. U of California, Berkeley, 1984.

———. "Desire and Presence: Bettine von Arnim's Erotic Fantasy Letter to Goethe." *Michigan Germanic Studies* 13.1 (1987): 41–57.

Gottschall, Rudolph. "Die Coeurdame der romantischen Schule." *Blätter für literarische Unterhaltung* 37 (1871): 577–83.

Graff, Harvey J. *The Literacy Myth: Literacy and Social Structure in the Nineteenth-Century City.* New York: Academic P, 1979.

Gries, Frauke. "Bettina von Arnim: A 'Romantic' Writer Foreshadowing Women of the Twentieth Century." *Simone de Beauvoir Studies* 10 (1993): 175–79.

Gumbrecht, Hans Ulrich. "The Role of Narration in Narrative Genres." *Making Sense in Life and Literature.* Trans. Glen Burns. Theory and History of Literature 79. Minneapolis: U of Minnesota P, 1992. 41–53.

Gundelfinger, Friedrich, ed. *Romantiker-Briefe.* Jena: Diederichs, 1907.

Günderrode, Karoline von. *Gedichte.* Ed. Franz Joseph Görtz. Frankfurt: Insel, 1985.

———. *Der Schatten eines Traumes: Gedichte, Prosa, Briefe, Zeugnisse von Zeitgenossen.* Ed. Christa Wolf. Darmstadt: Luchterhand, 1979.

Guilloton, Doris Starr. "Rahel Varnhagen und die Frauenfrage in der deutschen Romantik: Eine Untersuchung ihrer Briefe und Tagebuchnotizen." *Monatshefte* 69 (1977): 391–403.

———. "Toward a New Freedom: Rahel Varnhagen and the German Women Writers before 1848." *Woman as Mediatrix: Essays on Nineteenth-Century European Women Writers.* Ed. Avriel H. Goldberger. New York: Greenwood, 1987. 133–43.

Hahn, Barbara. "Brief und Werk: Zur Konstitution von Autorschaft um 1800." *Autorschaft: Genus und Genie in der Zeit um 1800*. Geschlechterdifferenz & Literatur 1. Ed. Ina Schabert and Barbara Schaff. Berlin: Schmidt, 1994. 145–56.

——, ed. *"Im Schlaf bin ich wacher": Die Träume der Rahel Levin Varnhagen*. Frankfurt: Luchterhand, 1990.

——. "'Weiber verstehen alles à la lettre': Briefkultur im beginnenden 19. Jahrhundert." Brinker-Gabler, *Deutsche Literatur* 2: 13–27.

Hahn, Barbara, and Ursula Isselstein, eds. *Rahel Levin Varnhagen: Die Wiederentdeckung einer Schriftstellerin*. LiLi: Zeitschrift für Literaturwissenschaft und Linguistik 14. Ed. Helmut Kreuzer. Göttingen: Vandenhoeck, 1987.

Hamann, Johann Georg. *Briefwechsel*. Ed. Walther Ziesemer and Arthur Henkel. 7 vols. Wiesbaden (vols. 1–4); Frankfurt (vols. 5–7): Insel, 1955–1979.

Härtl, Heinz. "Entstehungsgeschichte, biographischer, und zeitgeschichtlicher Umkreis." Arnim, *Werke* 1: 629–71.

Härtl, Heinz and Hartwig Schultz, eds. *"Die Erfahrung anderer Länder": Beiträge eines Wiepersdorfer Kolloquiums zu Achim und Bettina von Arnim*. New York: de Gruyter, 1994.

Haym, Rudolf. *Die romantische Schule: Ein Beitrag zur Geschichte des deutschen Geistes*. Berlin: Weidmann, 1920.

Heilbrun, Carolyn G. *Writing a Woman's Life*. New York: Ballantine, 1988.

Herminghouse, Patricia. "Women and the Literary Enterprise in Nineteenth-Century Germany." Joeres and Maynes 78–93.

Hertz, Deborah. *Jewish High Society in Old Regime Berlin*. New Haven: Yale UP, 1988.

——. "The Varnhagen Collection is in Krakow[!]" *American Archivist* 44 (1981): 223–28.

Herz, Henriette. *Henriette Herz in Erinnerung, Briefen, und Zeugnissen*. Ed. Rainer Schmitz. Frankfurt: Insel, 1984.

Heynen, Walter, ed. *Das Buch deutscher Briefe*. Wiesbaden: Insel, 1957.

Hirsch, Helmut. *Bettine von Arnim*. Reinbek bei Hamburg: Rowohlt, 1987.

Hoffmann, Leonore, and Margo Culley, eds. *Women's Personal Narratives: Essays in Criticism and Pedagogy*. New York: MLA, 1985.

Homans, Margaret. *Bearing the Word: Language and Female Experience in Nineteenth-Century Women's Writing*. Chicago: Chicago UP, 1986.

——. *Women Writers and Poetic Identity: Dorothy Wordsworth, Emily Brontë, and Emily Dickinson*. Princeton: Princeton UP, 1980.

Huch, Ricarda. *Gesammelte Werke*. Ed. Wilhelm Emrich. 11 vols. Cologne: Kiepenheuer and Witsch, 1966–74.

———. *Die Romantik: Blütezeit, Ausbreitung, und Verfall.* 1908–11. Tübingen: Wunderlich, 1951.

Isselstein, Ursula. "'Dies ist die Beute!': Zu Rahel Levins Tagebüchern." Hahn and Isselstein 86–103.

———. "Rahels Schriften I: Karl August Varnhagens editorische Tätigkeit nach Dokumenten seines Archivs." Hahn and Isselstein 16–32.

———. "'. . . daß ich kein Träumender allein hier bin!': Zwei unbekannte Träume Rahel Levins." *MLN* 102 (1987): 648–54.

———. *"Der Text aus meinem beleidigten Herzen": Studien zu Rahel Levin Varnhagen.* Collana di Lingua e Letteratura Straniera. Turin: Tirrenia, 1993.

Jäckel, Günther, ed. *Frauen der Goethezeit in ihren Briefen.* Berlin: Nation, 1966.

Jäckel, Günther, and Manfred Schlösser, eds. *Das Volk braucht Licht: Frauen zur Zeit des Aufbruchs 1790–1848 in ihren Briefen.* Darmstadt: Agora, 1970.

Jelinek, Estelle C. *The Tradition of Women's Autobiography: From Antiquity to the Present.* Boston: Twayne, 1986.

Joeres, Ruth-Ellen B., and Mary Jo Maynes, eds. *German Women in the Eighteenth and Nineteenth Centuries: A Social and Literary History.* Bloomington: Indiana UP, 1986.

Joeres, Ruth-Ellen B. "Self-Conscious Histories: Biographies of German Women in the Nineteenth Century." *German Women in the Nineteenth Century: A Social History.* Ed. John C. Fout. New York: Holmes and Meier, 1984. 172–96.

———. "'We are adjacent to human society': German Women Writers, the Homosocial Experience, and a Challenge to the Public / Domestic Dichotomy." *Women in German Yearbook: Feminist Studies in German Literature & Culture* 10 (1995): 39–57.

Johnson, Barbara. *A World of Difference.* Baltimore: Johns Hopkins UP, 1987.

Jurgensen, Manfred. *Das fiktionale Ich: Untersuchungen zum Tagebuch.* Bern: Francke, 1979.

———. *Women, Writers, Women Writers: An Alternative History of German Literature.* U of Queensland Inaugural Lectures. Queensland, Austral.: U of Queensland P, 1984.

Kahn, Lothar. "Heine's Jewish Writer Friends: Dilemma of a Generation, 1817–33." *The Jewish Response to German Culture: From the Enlightenment to the Second World War.* Ed. Jehuda Reinharz and Walter Schatzberg. Hanover, NH: UP of New England, 1985. 120–36.

Kahn-Wallerstein, Carmen. *Bettine: Die Geschichte eines ungestümen Herzens.* Bern: Francke, 1952.

Kauffman, Linda S. *Discourses of Desire: Gender, Genre, and Epistolary Fictions.* Ithaca: Cornell UP, 1986.

Kelling, Hans-Wilhelm. "Bettina von Arnim: A Study in Goethe Idolatry." *Rocky Mountain Review of Language and Literature* 23 (1969): 73–82.

Keul, Hildegund. *Menschwerden durch Berührung: Bettine Brentano-Arnim als Wegbereiterin für eine feministische Theologie.* New York: Lang, 1993.

Kleßmann, Eckart. *Caroline: Das Leben der Caroline Michaelis-Böhmer-Schlegel-Schelling 1763–1809.* Munich: List, 1975.

Kluckhohn, Paul. "Bettina von Arnim geb. Brentano (1785–1859)." *Neue Deutsche Biographie.* 4 vols. Berlin: Duncker, 1953. 1: 369–71.

Koch, Willi A., ed. *Briefe deutscher Romantiker.* Leipzig: Dieterich, 1938.

Kundera, Milan. *Immortality.* Trans. Peter Kussi. New York: Grove-Weidenfeld, 1991. Trans. of *Nesmrtelnost.* 1990.

Lacan, Jacques. "Seminar on *The Purloined Letter.*" *Yale French Studies* 48 (1972): 38–72.

Lennox, Sara. *Christa Wolf and the Women Romantics.* Studies in GDR Culture and Society 2. Washington, DC: UP of America, 1982.

———. "Trends in Literary Theory: The Female Aesthetic and German Women's Writing." *German Quarterly* 54.1 (1981): 63–75.

Liebertz-Grün, Ursula. *Ordnung im Chaos: Studien zur Poetik der Bettine Brentano-von Arnim.* Heidelberg: Winter, 1989.

Lilienfein, Heinrich. *Bettina von Arnim: Dichtung und Wahrheit ihres Lebens.* Munich: Bruckmann, 1949.

Lürßen, Johanna. *Die Frauen der Romantik.* Quellenhefte zum Frauenleben in der Geschichte 16. Ed. Emmy Beckmann and Irma Stoß. Berlin: Herbig, 1932.

Lüthi, Kurt. *Feminismus und Romantik: Sprache, Gesellschaft, Symbole, Religion.* Literatur und Leben 26. Vienna: Böhlaus, 1985.

MacArthur, Elizabeth J. *Extravagant Narratives: Closure and Dynamics in the Epistolary Form.* Princeton: Princeton UP, 1990.

Mander, Gertrud. *Bettina von Arnim.* Berlin: Stapp, 1982.

Manley, Mary Delarivière. *Memoirs of the Life of Mrs. Manley, Author of the Atalantis.* 1714. New York: AMS, 1976.

Martini, Fritz. *Deutsche Literaturgeschichte von den Anfängen bis zur Gegenwart.* Stuttgart: Kröner, 1984.

Mattenklot, Gert. "Romantische Frauenkultur: Bettina von Arnim zum Beispiel." Gnüg and Möhrmann 123–43.

Mauser, Wolfram, and Barbara Becker-Cantarino, eds. *Frauenfreundschaft—Männerfreundschaft: Literarische Diskurse im 18. Jahrhundert.* Tübingen: Niemeyer, 1991.

Mellor, Anne K., ed. *Romanticism and Feminism.* Bloomington: Indiana UP, 1988.

Menzel, Wolfgang. "Damen-Literatur." *Literatur-Blatt* 108 (1835): 429–32.

Meyer-Hepner, Gertrud. *Der Magistratsprozeß der Bettina von Arnim.* Ed. Helmut Hotzhauer and Karl-Heinz Klingenberg. Weimar: Arion, 1960.

Meyer-Krentler, Eckhardt. "Freundschaft im 18. Jahrhundert: Zur Einführung in die Forschungsdiskussion." Mauser and Becker-Cantarino 1–22.

Mielke, Gerda. *Caroline Schlegel nach ihren Briefen: Ein Beitrag zur Geistesgeschichte des 18. Jahrhunderts.* Diss. Greifswald U, 1925.

Milch, Werner. *Die junge Bettine, 1785–1811: Ein biographischer Versuch.* Heidelberg: Stiehm, 1968.

Miller, Nancy K. *Subject to Change: Reading Feminist Writing.* New York: Columbia UP, 1988.

Misch, Georg. *Geschichte der Autobiographie.* 4 vols. Frankfurt: Schulte-Bulmke, 1949–1967.

Mommsen, Katharina. "Goethes Einstellung zur Frau in neuer Sicht." *Jahrbuch: Berliner wissenschaftliche Gesellschaft, E. V.* (1980): 37–64.

Montagu, Mary Wortley. *The Selected Letters of Lady Mary Wortley Montagu.* Ed. Robert Halsband. New York: St. Martin's, 1970.

Montefiore, Jan. *Feminism and Poetry: Language, Experience, Identity in Women's Writing.* London: Pandora, 1987.

Morris, John N. *Versions of the Self: Studies in English Autobiography from John Bunyan to John Stuart Mill.* New York: Basic Books, 1966.

Murray, Janice. Introduction to "Caroline Schlegel-Schelling (1763–1809)." In Blackwell and Zantop, 281–84.

Nägele, Rainer. *Reading after Freud: Essays on Goethe, Hölderlin, Habermas, Nietzsche, Brecht, Celan, and Freud.* New York: Columbia UP, 1987.

Nickisch, Reinhard M. G. *Brief.* Stuttgart: Metzler, 1991.

———. "Briefkultur: Entwicklung und sozialgeschichtliche Bedeutung des Frauenbriefs im 18. Jahrhundert." Brinker-Gabler, *Deutsche Literatur* 1: 389–409.

———. *Die Stilprinzipien in den deutschen Briefstellern des 17. und 18. Jahrhunderts.* Palaestra 254. Göttingen: Vandenhoeck & Ruprecht, 1969.

Nussbaum, Felicity A. "Eighteenth-Century Women's Autobiographical Commonplaces." *The Private Self: Theory and Practice of Women's Autobiographical Writings.* Ed. Shari Benstock. Chapel Hill: U of North Carolina P, 1988. 147–71.

Ockenfuss, Solveig. *Bettine von Arnims Briefromane: Literarische Erinnerungsarbeit zwischen Anspruch und Wirklichkeit.* Opladen: Westdeutscher, 1992.

Oehlke, Waldemar. *Bettina von Arnims Briefromane.* Berlin: Mayer and Müller, 1905.

Olney, James. *Metaphors of Self: The Meaning of Autobiography*. Princeton: Princeton UP, 1972.

Panke-Kochinke, Birgit. *Die anständige Frau: Konzeption und Umsetzung bürgerlicher Moral im 18. und 19. Jahrhundert*. Frauen in Geschichte und Gesellschaft 31. Pfaffenweiler: Centaurus, 1991.

———. "Bürgerliches Frauenbild und Geschlechtsrollenzuweisungen in der literarischen und brieflichen Produktion des 18. Jahrhunderts." *Beiträge fünf zur feministischen Theorie und Praxis*. Munich: Frauenoffensive, 1981. 6–11.

Patsch, Hermann. "'Als ob Spinoza sich wollte taufen lassen': Biographisches und Rechtsgeschichtliches zu Taufe und Trauung Rahel Levins." *JFDH* (1991): 149–78.

———. "'Ob ich dich liebe, weiß ich nicht': Goethe und ein Wechselgedicht zwischen Bettina von Arnim und Friedrich Schleiermacher." *Zeitschrift für deutsche Philologie* 104 (1985): 542–54.

Paulsen, Wolfgang, ed. *Die Frau als Heldin und Autorin: Neue kritische Ansätze zur deutschen Literatur*. Bern: Francke, 1979.

Pazi, Margarita. "Rahel Varnhagen im Ganzen." *Neue Deutsche Hefte* 32 (1985): 562–66.

Porte, Joel. *In Respect to Egotism: Studies in American Romantic Writing*. Cambridge: Cambridge UP, 1991.

Prokop, Ulrike. "Die Freundschaft zwischen Katharina Elisabeth Goethe und Bettina Brentano — Aspekte weiblicher Tradition." Mauser and Becker-Cantarino 237–77.

Püschel, Ursula. '— *wider die Philister und die bleierne Zeit': Untersuchungen, Essays, Aufsätze über Bettina von Arnim*. Berlin: Altberliner Bücherstube, Verlagsbuchhandlung Seifert, 1996.

Ritchie, Gisela F. *Caroline Schlegel-Schelling in Wahrheit und Dichtung*. Bonn: Bouvier, 1968.

Ronell, Avital. "Goethezeit." *Taking Chances: Derrida, Psychoanalysis, and Literature*. Ed. Joseph H. Smith, William Kerrigan, and Jacques Derrida. Baltimore: Johns Hopkins UP, 1984. 146–82.

Ross, Marlon B. "Romantic Quest and Conquest: Troping Masculine Power in the Crisis of Poetic Identity." Mellor 26–51.

Rothmund, Toni. *Caroline Schlegel*. Leipzig: Reclam, 1926.

Runge, Anita and Lieselotte Steinbrügge, eds. *Die Frau im Dialog: Studien zu Theorie und Geschichte des Briefes*. Ergebnisse der Frauenforschung 21. Stuttgart: Metzler, 1991.

Salinas, Pedro. *Verteidigung des Briefes: Ein Essay*. 1954. Trans. Wilhelm Muster. Frankfurt: Klett-Cotta-Ullstein, 1983.

Scherer, Wilhelm. *Geschichte der deutschen Literatur*. Berlin: Weidmann, 1880–82.

Schiller, Friedrich. *Briefe*. Ed. Karl-Heinz Hahn. 2 vols. Berlin: Aufbau, 1982.

———. *Briefe*. Ed. Erwin Streitfeld und Viktor Z'megat. Königstein, Czech.: Athenäum, 1983.

Schiller, Friedrich, and Johann Wolfgang Goethe. *Der Briefwechsel zwischen Schiller und Goethe*. Ed. Emil Staiger. Frankfurt: Insel, 1977.

Schlaffer, Hannelore. "Frauen als Einlösung der romantischen Kunsttheorie." *Jahrbuch der deutschen Schillergesellschaft* 7 (1977): 274–96.

Schlegel, Friedrich. *Friedrich Schlegels Briefe an seinen Bruder August Wilhelm*. Ed. Oskar Walzel. Berlin: Speyer, 1890.

———. *Kritische Friedrich-Schlegel-Ausgabe*. 35 vols. expected. Ed. Ernst Behler et al. Munich: Schöningh, 1958- .

Schlegel-Schelling, Caroline (also cited as Karoline Michaelis, Schlegel, or Schelling). *Caroline: Briefe an ihre Geschwister, ihre Tochter Auguste, die Familie Gotter, F. L. W. Meyer, A. W. und Fr. Schlegel, J. Schelling u. a. nebst Briefen von A. W. und Fr. Schlegel u. a.* Ed. Georg Waitz. 2 vols. Leipzig: Hirzel, 1871.

———. *Caroline: Briefe aus der Frühromantik*. Ed. Erich Schmidt. 2 vols. Leipzig: Insel, 1913. Rpt. Berlin: Lang, 1970.

———. *Caroline und Dorothea Schlegel in Briefen*. Ed. Ernst Wieneke. Weimar: Kiepenheuer, 1914.

———. *Caroline und ihre Freunde: Mittheilungen aus Briefen*. Ed. Georg Waitz. Leipzig: Hirzel, 1882.

———. *Carolinens Leben in ihren Briefen*. Ed. Reinhard Buchwald. Intro. Ricarda Huch. Leipzig: Insel, 1914.

———. *Karoline Michaelis: Eine Auswahl ihrer Briefe*. Ed. Helene Stöcker. Berlin: Oesterheld, 1912.

———. *Caroline Schlegel-Schelling "Lieber Freund, ich komme weit her schon an diesem frühen Morgen": Briefe*. Ed. Sigrid Damm. Darmstadt: Luchterhand, 1980.

———. *Unruhvolles Herz: Briefe der Caroline Schelling*. Ed. Willi A. Koch. Ebenhausen bei München: Brandt, 1951.

Schormann, Sabine. *Bettine von Arnim: Die Bedeutung Schleiermachers für ihr Leben und Werk*. Tübingen: Niemeyer, 1993.

Schmitz, Walter, and Sybille von Steinsdorff, eds. *Der Geist muß Freiheit genießen — : Studien zu Werk und Bildungsprogramm Bettine von Arnims*. Bettina von Arnim-Studien 2. Berlin: FSP Saint Albain, 1992.

Schuller, Marianne. "Dialogisches Schreiben: Zum literarischen Umfeld Rahel Levin Varnhagens." Hahn and Isselstein 173–86.

Schultz, Hans Jürgen, ed. *Frauen: Porträts aus zwei Jahrhunderten*. Stuttgart: Kreuz, 1981.

Schumann, Sabine. "Das 'lesende Frauenzimmer': Frauenzeitschriften im 18. Jahrhundert." Becker-Cantarino, *Die Frau* 138–69.

Schweikert, Uwe. "Am jüngsten Tag' hab ich recht": Rahel Varnhagen als Briefschreiberin." Varnhagen, *Gesammelte Werke* 10: 17–42.

Scurla, Herbert. *Begegnungen mit Rahel: Der Salon der Rahel Levin*. Berlin: Nation, 1962.

Seibert, Peter. *Der literarische Salon: Literatur und Geselligkeit zwischen Aufklärung und Vormärz*. Stuttgart: Metzler, 1993.

Seidel, Ina. *Bettina*. Stuttgart: Cotta, 1944.

———. *Drei Dichter der Romantik: Clemens Brentano, Bettina, Achim von Arnim*. Stuttgart: Deutsche Verlags-Anstalt, 1944.

Showalter, Elaine. "Feminist Criticism in the Wilderness." *Writing and Sexual Difference*. Ed. Elizabeth Abel. Chicago: U of Chicago P, 1982. 9–35.

———. *A Literature of Their Own: British Women Novelists from Brontë to Lessing*. Princeton: Princeton UP, 1977.

———, ed. *The New Feminist Criticism: Essays on Women, Literature, and Theory*. New York: Pantheon, 1985.

Sidgwick, Mrs. Alfred [Cecily]. *Caroline Schlegel and Her Friends*. New York: Scribner and Welford, 1889.

Smith, Sidonie. *A Poetics of Women's Autobiography: Marginality and the Fictions of Self-Representation*. Bloomington: Indiana UP, 1987.

Spacks, Patricia Meyer. *The Female Imagination*. New York: Knopf, 1975.

———. "Female Resources: Epistles, Plot, and Power." Goldsmith 63–76.

———. *Imagining a Self: Autobiography and Novel in Eighteenth-Century England*. Cambridge: Harvard UP, 1976.

Spender, Dale. *Mothers of the Novel: One Hundred Good Women Writers before Jane Austen*. London: Pandora, 1986.

Spengemann, William C. *The Forms of Autobiography: Episodes in the History of a Literary Genre*. New Haven: Yale UP, 1980.

Spiel, Hilde. "Rahel Varnhagen: Tragic Muse of the Romantics." *Affairs of the Mind: The Salon in Europe and America from the 18th to the 20th Century*. Ed. Peter Quennell. Washington, D.C.: New Republic, 1980. 13–21.

Stanton, Domna C. "Autogynography: Is the Subject Different?" *The Female Autograph: Theory and Practice of Autobiography from the Tenth to the Twentieth Century*. Ed. Domna C. Stanton and Jeanine Parisier Plottel. Chicago: U of Chicago P, 1984. 3–20.

Steig, Reinhold, and Herman Grimm, eds. *Achim von Arnim und die ihm nahe standen*. 3 vols. Stuttgart: Cotta, 1894–1913.

Steinhausen, Georg. *Geschichte des deutschen Briefes: Zur Kulturgeschichte des deutschen Volkes.* 1889–91. Zurich: Weidmann, 1968.

Stern, Ludwig. *Die Varnhagen von Ensesche Sammlung in der Königlichen Bibliothek in Berlin.* Berlin: Behrend, 1911.

Stieglitz, Charlotte. *Gedichte und Briefe.* Frankfurt: Insel, 1987.

Stimpson, Catharine R. "Ad / d Feminam: Women, Literature, and Society." *Literature and Society.* Ed. Edward W. Said. Baltimore: Johns Hopkins UP, 1980. 174–92.

Susman, Margarete. *Frauen der Romantik.* Jena: Diederichs, 1929.

Tanneberger, Irmgard. *Die Frauen der Romantik und das soziale Problem.* Oldenberg: Schwartz, 1928.

Tatlock, Lynne. "The Young Germans in Praise of Famous Women: Ambivalent Advocates." *German Life and Letters* 39 (1986): 193–209.

Tewarson, Heidi Thomann. "Caroline Schlegel and Rahel Varnhagen: The Response of Two German Women to the French Revolution and Its Aftermath." *Seminar: A Journal of Germanic Studies* 29.2 (1993): 106–24.

———. "German-Jewish Identity in the Correspondence between Rahel Levin Varnhagen and Her Brother, Ludwig Robert: Hopes and Realities of Emancipation, 1780–1830." *Leo Baeck Institute Yearbook* 39 (1994): 3–29.

———. "'Ich bin darin der erste Ignorant der Welt! der *dabei* so viel auf Kenntnisse hält': Zum Bildungsweg Rahel Levins." Hahn and Isselstein 141–51.

———. "Jüdisches-Weibliches: Rahel Levin Varnhagens Reisen als Überschreitungen." *German Quarterly* 66 (1993): 145–159.

———. *Rahel Levin Varnhagen.* Reinbek bei Hamburg: Rowohlt, 1988.

Thalmann, Marianne. *Romantik und Manierismus.* Stuttgart: Kohlhammer, 1963.

Thielenhaus, Vera. "Die 'Göttinger Sieben' und Bettine von Arnims Eintreten für die Brüder Grimm." *Internationales Jahrbuch der Bettina-von-Arnim Gesellschaft* 5 (1993): 54–72.

Todorov, Tzvetan. *Genres in Discourse.* 1978. Trans. Catherine Porter. Cambridge: Cambridge UP, 1990.

Varnhagen, Rahel (also cited as Rahel Levin or Robert). *Aus dem Nachlaß Varnhagen's von Ense: Briefwechsel zwischen Rahel und David Veit.* 2 vols. Ed. Ludmilla Assing. Leipzig: Brockhaus, 1861.

———. *Aus dem Nachlaß Varnhagen's von Ense: Briefwechsel zwischen Varnhagen und Rahel.* 6 vols. Ed. Ludmilla Assing. Leipzig: Brockhaus, 1874–75.

———. *Aus Rahel's Herzensleben: Briefe und Tagebuchblätter.* Ed. Ludmilla Assing. Leipzig: Brockhaus, 1877.

———. *Briefe an eine Freundin: Rahel Varnhagen an Rebecca Friedländer.* Ed. Deborah Hertz. Cologne: Kiepenheuer and Witsch, 1988.

———. *Briefwechsel.* 4 vols. Ed. Friedhelm Kemp. Munich: Kösel, 1966–68.

———. *Briefwechsel mit Pauline Wiesel.* Ed. Barbara Hahn. Munich: Beck, 1997.

———. *Briefwechsel zwischen Karoline von Humboldt, Rahel, und Varnhagen.* Ed. Albert Leitzmann. Weimar: Böhlau, 1896.

———. *Gallerie von Bildnissen aus Rahel's Umgang und Briefwechsel.* 2 vols. Ed. Karl August Varnhagen von Ense. Leipzig: Reichenbach, 1836.

———. *Gesammelte Werke.* 10 vols. Ed. Konrad Feilchenfeldt, Uwe Schweikert, and Rahel E. Steiner. Munich: Matthes and Seitz, 1983.

———. *Rahel: Ein Buch des Andenkens für ihre Freunde.* Ed. Karl August Varnhagen von Ense. Berlin: 1833.

———. *Rahel und Alexander von der Marwitz in ihren Briefen: Ein Bild aus der Zeit der Romantiker.* Ed. Heinrich Meisner. Gotha: Klotz, 1925.

———. *Rahel und ihre Zeit: Briefe und Zeugnisse.* Ed. Bertha Badt. Munich: Rentsch, 1912.

———. *Rahel Varnhagen: Ein Frauenleben in Briefen.* Ed. Augusta Weldler-Steinberg. Weimar: Kiepenheuer, 1912.

———. *Rahel Varnhagen: Jeder Wunsch wird Frivolität genannt.* Ed. Marlis Gerhardt. Darmstadt: Luchterhand, 1983.

Vigliero, Consolina. "'Verlassen Sie sich nicht selbst!': Zu einem ungedruckten Brief von Rahel Levin." *Leo Baeck Institute Bulletin* 77 (1987): 49–71.

Vordtriede, Werner, ed. *Bettina von Arnim's Armenbuch.* Frankfurt: Insel, 1969.

Waldeck, Peter B. *The Split Self from Goethe to Broch.* London: Associated UP, 1979.

Waldstein, Edith. *Bettine von Arnim and the Politics of Romantic Conversation.* Studies in German Literature, Linguistics, and Culture 33. Columbia, SC: Camden House, 1988.

Weigel, Sigrid. *Die verborgene Frau: Sechs Beiträge zu einer feministischen Literaturwissenschaft.* Argument-Sonderband 96. Berlin: Argument, 1983.

Weissberg, Liliane. "Anders schreiben? Überlegungen zu Briefe Rahel Varnhagens an Friedrich de la Motte Fouqué: Im Auftrag des Schweizerischen Werkbundes." *Kanalarbeit: Medienstrategien im Kulturwandel.* Ed. Hans Ulrich Reck. Basel: Roter Stern, 1988. 148–62.

———. "Schreiben als Selbstentwurf: Zu den Schriften Rahel Varnhagens and Dorothea Schlegels." *Zeitschrift für Religions- und Geistesgeschichte* 47 (1995): 231–53.

———. "Selbstbeschreibung als pädagogischer Diskurs: Rahel Varnhagens Briefe." Hahn and Isselstein 76–85.

———. "Turns of Emancipation: On Rahel Varnhagen's Letters." Goodman and Waldstein 53–70.

———. "Writing on the Wall: Letters of Rahel Varnhagen." *New German Critique* 36 (1985): 157–73.

Weißenborn, Birgit. *Bettina von Arnim und Goethe: Topographie einer Beziehung als Beispiel weiblicher Emanzipation zu Beginn des 19. Jahrhunderts.* Frankfurt: Lang, 1987.

Westermann, Charlotte, ed. *Briefe der Liebe aus drei Jahrhunderten deutscher Vergangenheit.* Ebenhausen: Brandt, 1913.

Woodmansee, Martha. *The Author, Art and the Market: Rereading the History of Aesthetics.* New York: Columbia UP, 1994.

Zimmermann, Karin. *Die polyfunktionale Bedeutung dialogischer Sprechformen um 1800: Exemplarische Analysen: Rahel Varnhagen, Bettine von Arnim, Karoline Günderrode.* New York: Lang, 1992.

Index

address, epistolary form of, x, 10, 22, 32, 34, 38, 41–42, 59, 67, 77, 83, 93, 100, 102
Altman, Janet, 4, 22–23, 32, 68
androgyny, 6, 77, 96
anti-Semitism, 43, 46, 49
aphorism, 26, 53, 54, 55, 57, 60, 61, 66, 68, 71, 91
Arendt, Hannah, 7, 47, 54
Arnim, Bettina von, ix–xi, xii, 1–3, 6, 8, 9, 10, 12, 25, 74–103, 106, 107, 108;
  and her children, 78, 79, 85;
  and Goethe, 77–79, 81, 82–87, 88, 90–103;
  as a muse, 77;
  and salons, 74, 76, 79–80;
  and Schlegel-Schelling, 13, 20, 21, 22, 36, 39, 43–44, 50, 56, 74, 77, 79, 81, 87, 88, 94, 97;
  and the self, 12–13, 70;
  and Varnhagen, 13, 22, 36, 49, 50–52, 56, 70, 74, 77, 79, 80, 81, 87, 89, 93, 96, 97;
  works by:
  Bettina von Arnims Armenbuch, 80;
  Dies Buch gehört dem König, 80, 81;
  Clemens Brentano's Frühlingskranz, 76, 80, 81, 90;
  Goethes Briefwechsel mit einem Kinde, xii, 77, 79, 80, 81, 82–103, 106;
  Gespräche mit Dämonen, 80, 81;
  Die Günderode, 76, 80, 81, 90;
  Ilius Pamphilius und die Ambrosia, 80, 81, 87, 90;
  Sämtliche Schriften, 18
Arnim, Ludwig Achim von, xi, 75, 76, 77, 78, 79, 85, 86
Assing, Ludmilla, 53
Austen, Jane, 98
authorship, 9, 12, 24, 51, 61–65, 87
autobiography, 5, 11–12, 23, 32–33, 38, 52, 56–57, 60, 61, 64, 66–67, 71, 78

Barnouw, Dagmar, 4
Beauvoir, Simone de, 105, 108–109
Becker–Cantarino, Barbara, 3, 24
Beethoven, Ludwig van, ix, 53, 79
Behrens, Katja, 3
Bertuch, Wilhelmina, 15, 22, 34, 35, 37
Biedermeier, 88
biography, 5, 7, 11, 21, 28, 30, 36–38, 40–42, 66, 76, 82–83, 86, 92
Blackwell, Jeannine, 3, 47
Böhmer, Auguste, 17, 19, 39, 40, 42–43
Böhmer, George, 17
Böhmer, Johann Franz Wilhelm, xi, 15–17, 30, 35, 37, 39
Böhmer, Therese, 17, 40
Boswell, James, xi
Bovenschen, Sylvia, 10
Boye, Antonie, 61
Brahms, Johannes, 79

Brentano, Bettine, see: Arnim, Bettina von
Brentano, Clemens, 48, 50, 59, 75, 76, 80, 84–87, 90, 94, 96, 97, 98
Brentano, Maximiliane von La Roche, 74, 96, 98
Brentano, Peter Anton, 74
Brinckmann, Karl Gustav von, 48, 60, 61, 62
Brinker-Gabler, Gisela, 90
Brun-Münter, Friederike, 23
Buchwald, Reinhard, 27, 29
Bürger, Christa, 58, 66–67

canon, 1, 2–3, 4–5, 8, 21, 22, 47
Catholicism, Roman, 74, 75
Chamisso, Adelbert, 48
Cixous, Hélène, 6, 34
Coleridge, Samuel Taylor, 33
conversation, 5–7, 15, 33, 39, 48, 49, 52, 57, 58, 78, 92, 100
Cook, Captain James, 17
Corngold, Stanley, 11, 33, 34
correspondence, xi, 1, 4–13, 20–22, 27, 30, 45, 54–55, 59–64, 66–69, 71, 76, 80–81, 88–92, 94;
  defined as a genre, 4–5, 106–109
Creuzer, Friedrich, 76

Daley, Margaretmary, 100
Damm, Sigrid, 3, 27, 29
Dante, 47
death, 37, 39–40, 42–43, 45, 70, 71–72, 85, 93, 95, 99, 108
Derrida, Jacques, 34
dialogue, 2, 10, 26, 60, 66–72, 94, 108, 109
diary, xi, 22, 23, 54, 60, 66, 67, 69, 71, 90, 95, 102, 103, 105
Dickinson, Emily, 56
Diderot, Denis, 47

Dilthey, Wilhelm, 30
Dischner, Gisela, 7, 29, 37
Dubois-Crancé, Jean-Baptiste, 17, 29, 30
Du-Form, see: address, form of

écriture féminine, 6
egocentricity, see: self, egocentric
Elsholtz, Karl, 62–63, 65
epistolarity, ix, 3–13, 22–23, 26, 38–39, 55, 59–62, 66–68, 80, 87, 88–92, 98, 99, 107–109;
  epistolary narrative, xi, 13, 29, 30–33;
  epistolary novel, xi, 2, 5, 7, 12, 83, 88, 89, 98, 103
eroticism, 6, 84, 103

Feilchenfeldt, Konrad, xii, 53–54, 60, 88
feminist criticism, x, 6, 33–34, 75
Fichte, Johann Gottlieb, 42, 44, 47, 67
Finckenstein, Count Karl Finck von, 49, 50, 51, 61
flesh, 83, 84, 94
Forster, Georg, 17, 18, 25, 30, 39
Forster-Huber, Therese Heyne, 16, 17
Fouqué, Karoline von, 50
Frederiksen, Elke, 4, 6
French Revolution, x, 17–18, 20, 76
French, Lorely, 3, 33, 107
Friedländer, Rebecca, xii, 50, 54
Friedrichsmeyer, Sara, 3, 14
friendship, 15, 21, 24, 31, 52, 57, 59–60, 66, 68, 71, 74, 77, 93, 95, 105, 107;
female friendship, 32, 35–36, 50, 66, 76, 92, 93
Frühwald, Wolfgang, 8
Fuller, Margaret, 33

Gans, Eduard, 52
Gellert, Christian, 4, 9–10, 36, 39
gender, 1–11, 24, 26, 32, 58, 65, 84–87, 96, 106, 107
Genette, Girard, 11
genre, i–ii, xi, 1–11, 22–27, 30, 32–33, 34–35, 66–73, 87, 88, 91, 107; see also: autobiography, biography, correspondence, epistolary novel
Gentz, Friedrich von, 48
Gerhardt, Marlis, 3
Gilbert, Sandra, 6
Gleim, Johann Wilhelm Ludwig, 18
God, 18, 35, 68–69, 97
Goethe, Christiane, 78, 95
Goethe, Elisabeth, 77, 86, 90, 91, 92, 93, 96, 99, 103
Goethe, Johann Wolfgang von, ix, 2, 7, 9, 13, 14, 19, 39, 47, 63, 68, 69, 72, 78, 80, 81, 88, 89, 106;
  and Arnim, 77–79, 82–87, 90–103;
  and Schlegel-Schelling, 77;
  and Varnhagen, 77;
  works by:
  Briefwechsel zwischen Schiller und Goethe, 10;
  Die Leiden des jungen Werthers, 74, 100;
  Erwin und Elmire, 34;
  Faust II, 85–86;
  Hermann und Dorothea, 66, 98;
  Iphigenie auf Tauris, 23, 34, 98;
  "Mahomet's Song," 98;
  Torquato Tasso, 49;
  Wilhelm Meisters Lehrjahre, 49, 51, 75, 77, 98
Goodman, Katherine R., 3, 4

Goozé, Marjanne Elain, 88
Gotter, Luise Stieler, ix, 15, 16, 19, 22, 23, 24, 28, 32, 34, 35–36, 37, 39, 41, 43, 44, 50
Gottsched, Luise, 107
Grimm, Jakob and Wilhelm, 80, 106
Gubar, Susan, 6
Gumbrecht, Hans Ulrich, 11
Günderrode, Karoline von, 33, 39, 76, 77, 91, 93, 96, 103, 107
Gutzkow, Karl, 59

Hahn, Barbara, 24, 54, 58
Hamann, Johann Georg, 25
Härtl, Heinz, 81, 85, 86
Haym, Rudolf, 30
Hegel, Georg Wilhelm Friedrich, 52, 53, 64
Heilbrun, Carolyn G., 105, 107
Heine, Heinrich, 52, 59
Heineman, Daniel, 82
Hertz, Deborah, 5, 54
Herz, Henriette Lemos, 16, 48, 107
Heyne, Therese, see: Forster-Huber, Therese Heyne
Hirsch, Helmut, xii
Hölderlin, Friedrich, 6
Homans, Margaret, 24
Homer, 47
Horn, Antonie von, 64, 65
Huber, Therese, see: Forster-Huber, Therese Heyne
Huch, Ricarda, 4, 7, 18, 29
Humboldt, Alexander von, 52
Humboldt, Karoline von, xii, 19, 53, 63, 64
Humboldt, Wilhelm von, 4, 47
Hume, David, 47

identity, 2, 84, 94–95, 103, 108, 109

International Bettina von Arnim Society, 3
Isselstein, Ursula, 54, 62–63
Jäckel, Günther, 3
Jacobi, Johann Georg, 47
Jelinek, Estelle C., 32
Jena Romantics, 19–20, 34, 44, 79, 97
Jewishness, x, 46–48, 49, 50, 53, 54, 55, 56, 58, 59, 108
Joeres, Ruth-Ellen B., 3, 82
Johnson, Barbara, 7
Jurgensen, Manfred, 34

Karl August, Duke of Saxon-Weimar, 78
Kauffman, Linda S., 4, 23, 33, 68
Kelling, Hans-Wilhelm, 82
Kleist, Heinrich von, 50, 67
Kleßmann, Eckart, 14, 34, 42
Koch, Willi A., 27
Konrad, Gustav, 81
Krantz, Wilhelm Julius, 18
Kundera, Milan, 82

La Roche, Sophie von, 18, 25, 74, 75, 76, 87, 90, 98
Lessing, Gotthold Ephraim, 14, 47
letter writing, see: correspondence
Levin, Chaie, 47
Levin, Marcus, (father to Rahel), 47
Levin, Markus, (brother to Rahel), 47
Lichtenberg, Georg Christoph, 14
Louis Ferdinand, Prince, 48
love, x, 15, 18, 19, 24, 29, 30, 35–39, 43–45, 64, 68, 70, 77, 78, 83–90, 91–92, 93–103;
love letters, 38–39, 42, 43, 77, 83–84, 94, 101, 103
Lürßen, Johanna, 4
Lüthi, Kurt, 37

MacArthur, Elizabeth, 4
Mähl, Hans-Joachim, 8
Marwitz, Alexander von der, 49, 67, 69
Maynes, Mary Jo, 3
memoirs, 11, 22, 32, 51, 66
Mendelssohn, Fanny, 79
Mendelssohn, Felix, 79
Mendelssohn, Moses, 47, 48
Mereau, Sophie, 33
Meyer, Friedrich, ix, 28, 30, 32, 40–42
Meyer-Hepner, Gertrud, 87
Michaelis, Johann David, 14
Michaelis, Lotte, 31, 32, 37, 38
Michaelis, Phillip, 18, 39
Miller, Nancy K., 105
Mirabeau, Honoré-Gabriel Riqueti, comte de, 76
monolog, 16, 32, 60, 67
Montagu, Lady Mary Wortley, 23, 90
Montaigne, Michel Eyquem de, 47
Moritz, Karl Philipp, 34
Müller, Joachim, 81, 98
Müller-Seidel, Walter, 8
Murray, Janice, 3, 14

Nägele, Rainer, 71–72
Napoleon, 50, 51
Nickisch, Reinhard, 26, 33, 61
Nicolai, Friedrich, 47
nomenclature, confusion in, xi, 14, 55, 75
Novalis, 34, 106

Oehlke, Waldemar, 81, 92

Paul, Jean (Jean Paul Friedrich Richter), 34, 47
Pepys, Samuel, xi
Porte, Joel, 10
private v. public, 21, 52, 87, 105, 106

Pückler-Muskau, Hermann Fürst von, 81, 91

Radziwill, Prince, 48
Ramler, Karl Wilhelm, 47
Ranke, Leopold, 52
Ritchie, Gisela F., 14, 36
Robert, Ludwig, xi, 60, 64, 69
Romanticism, German, ix, xi, 3, 4, 7, 9, 10, 12, 14, 34, 44, 53, 84, 88, 106, 108
Rothmund, Toni, 34
Rottenhof, Friederike Anna von, 75
Rousseau, Jean-Jacques, 47, 75, 77

Saint-Simonism, 53
salons, ix, x, 5–6, 18, 18–20, 21, 46, 48–49, 50–52, 55, 56, 57, 59, 64, 70, 74, 76, 79, 80
Schelling, Friedrich Wilhelm Joseph, ix, xi, 14, 19, 20, 26, 28, 37, 38, 42, 43, 44
Schelling, Karoline, see: Schlegel-Schelling, Caroline
Schiller, Friedrich, 4, 7, 19, 21, 34, 47, 57, 82;
  works by:
  Ästhetische Briefe über die Erziehung des Menschen, 25;
  Briefwechsel zwischen Goethe und Schiller, 10;
  "Die Glocke," 18;
  Maria Stuart, 23
Schlegel, August Wilhelm, ix, xi, 14, 18, 19, 20, 24, 25–26, 38, 40, 42–44;
  works by:
  Athenäum, 26;
  Lucinda, 26;
  "On Philosophy: To Dorothea," 25

Schlegel, Dorothea Mendelssohn Veit, see Dorothea Veit
Schlegel, Friedrich, xi, 19, 26, 47, 48, 94, 97, 106
Schlegel-Schelling, Caroline, xii–xi, xii, 1, 8, 10, 14–45, 90, 94, 100, 106, 107, 108;
  and Arnim, 13, 21, 22, 36, 43, 50, 56, 74, 77, 79, 81, 87, 88, 94, 97, 100;
  and editorial issues, 8, 20, 27–31;
  education of, 14–15;
  marriage to Böhmer, 15–16;
  and Goethe, 77;
  marriage to Schelling, 19–20;
  marriage to Schlegel, 18–20;
  and letter writing, 21–27;
  and politics, 17–18;
  and the self, 12–13;
  and salons, 18–20, 21;
  and Varnhagen, 12, 13, 21, 22, 36, 50, 55, 56, 62–63, 74, 77, 79, 81, 88;
  works by:
  Caroline: Briefe an ihre Geschwister... ix–x, xii, 28;
  Caroline: Briefe aus der Frühromantik, xii, 20–22, 27–31, 33–45
Schleiermacher, Friedrich, 51, 53, 85, 86
Schlözer, Dorothea, 15
Schmidt, Erich, xii, 27–28, 29–30, 35
Schmitz, Walter, xii, 81
Schumann, Robert, 79
Schweikert, Uwe, xii, 5–6, 53–54, 88
Scurla, Herbert, 5, 59
Seibert, Peter, 5
self, the x, xi, xii, 1, 5, 11, 12–13, 27, 39, 45, 53, 66–68, 71, 77–78, 82, 84, 88, 95, 98, 103;

egocentric self, 12, 55–60, 64, 66–73, 108;
female self, ix, xii, 7, 21–22, 45, 56, 60, 82;
written forms of the self, xi–xii, 1, 2, 4, 11–13, 32, 45, 105, 106, 108
self-celebration, 63, 68, 83, 108
self-definition, ix, xi, 64, 82
self-discovery, ix, xi, 2, 4, 10, 12, 32, 35, 60, 74, 82, 84, 103, 107, 109
self-effacement, 60, 68, 87, 94
self-expression, ix, 1, 2, 4, 7, 10–13, 22, 27, 42, 55–56, 60, 63, 68, 71, 105–109
self-fashioning, xi, 77–78, 81, 88–91, 106
self-knowledge, 12, 67, 71
self-recognition, 64
self-vision, xii, 2, 12, 31, 95–96, 96–97, 108–109
Sévigné, Marie de Rabutin-Chantal marquise de, 90
Shafi, Monika, 6
Shakespeare, William, 6, 19, 24, 25, 26, 47
Showalter, Elaine, 6
Sidgwick, Cecily, 14
Spacks, Patricia Meyer, 7, 11, 12, 98, 100
Spengemann, William C., 66
Spinoza, Baruch, 44, 63, 67
Staël, Madame de, 20, 43
Stanton, Domna C., 33, 57
Steiner, Rahel E., xii, 53–54
Steinhausen, Georg, 61
Steinsdorff, Sibylle von, xii, 81
Stimpson, Catharine R., 3
Stöcker, Helene, 27, 29
Studnitz, Julie von, 16, 35, 36

Tanneberger, Irmgard, 4
Tasso, Torquato, 47

Tatter, Georg, 28, 40
Tewarson, Heidi Thomann, 3, 47, 54
Thurneisen, Karl Wilhelm, 34
Tieck, Ludwig, ix, 47, 48, 106
translation, x, 6, 20, 24, 26, 81, 82, 97

Urquijo, Don Rafael d', 49–50, 51, 61

Varnhagen, Karl August, xi, 50–55, 58, 60, 61–62, 64, 70, 80, 81, 82
Varnhagen, Rahel Levin, ix–xi, xii, 1, 3, 4, 5–6, 10, 33, 46–73, 106, 107, 108;
and Arnim, 13, 22, 36, 50, 52, 56, 70, 74, 77, 79, 80, 81, 87, 88, 89, 91, 93, 96;
as author, 60–65;
education, 47;
and Goethe, 49, 77;
love affairs, 49–50;
marriage, 51;
and salons, 48, 52, 55, 56, 57, 59, 64, 70;
and Schlegel-Schelling, 8, 12, 13, 21, 22, 36, 50, 55, 56, 62–63, 74, 77, 79, 81, 83;
and the self, 12–13, 55–60, 66–73;
works by:
"Fragments from Letters and Memorabilia," 51;
"On Goethe: Fragments taken from Letters," 51;
Rahel: Ein Buch des Andenkens für ihre Freunde, x, xii, 53–73;
editorial issues in, 53–55;
exploration of the self in, 55–60;
questions of genre, 66–73

Veit, David, xii, 53, 58
Veit, Dorothea Mendelssohn, 19, 43, 48, 107
Vigliero, Consolina, 69
voice, xi, 7, 33, 44, 52, 59, 60, 64, 88, 94, 96, 103, 107–109; female voice, 6, 7, 37, 106
Voltaire, 64, 65
Vordtriede, Werner, 93, 94

Waitz, Georg, ix, xii, 20, 27–28
Waldstein, Edith, 3, 91
Weigel, Sigrid, 24
Weissberg, Liliane, 5
Whitman, Walt, 64
Wiedemann, Luise, 28, 43
Wieland, Christoph Martin, 34, 47
Wieneke, Ernst, 27
Wiesel, Pauline, 48, 50, 54
Woodmansee, Martha, 87
Woolf, Virginia, 6, 21
Wordsworth, Dorothy, 24
Wordsworth, William, 9

Zantop, Susanne, 3, 47

OHIO UNIVERSITY LIBRARY

Please return this book as soon as you have finished with it. In order to avoid a fine it must be returned by the latest date stamped below. All books are subject to recall after two weeks or immediately if needed for reserve.

RETURN BY

NOV 10 1999

NOV 1 1999

CF